GW00506106

30130 127378650

THE HISTORIC TOWNS OF

NORFOLK, SUFFOLK AND ESSEX

JOHN BURGESS

CARLISLE

1991

ISBN 1 85562 027 8

E

INTRODUCTION

CONTENTS

Norfolk, Suffolk and Essex form what is
usualy described as East Anglia, that enormous
hump shaped region that sticks out towards Europe
on the eastern seaboard, bounded by the midlands in
the west, the sea in the east, the Wash to the north
and the Thames to the south. It is a region of
much diversity despite the usual idea that it
is all flat: there are many gentle hills, rolling
countryside, enormous beaches, expanses of mud and
estuary, plenty of woodland, substantial districts of
pasture and arable farming, seemingly endless villages,
and scores of small historic towns, and a few larger
and industrial ones. I first explored it as a sixth
former more than 20 years ago, and have returned many
times since to partake of its diversity of attractions:
being so handy for London, some of the towns and
the Broads (the manmade lakes) have become crowded:
but even so far more of the region is unspoiled by
tourism, and maintains the life of a prosperous provincial
place as it has done for a thousand years. Funnily
enough East Anglia has become increasingly popular for
migration to it from the south east - thus house prices
have soared, jobs multiplied as firms relocated in the
pleasanter Anglian atmosphere, and the region has become
in the space of 20 years one of the boom regions of
the nation. The historic towns are at the centre of
these changes.

NORFOLK

NORFOLK

GREAT YARMOUTH

        Norfolk is not very flat, in contradiction
to Noel Coward's ofte quoted remark: it has as many
gradients as one could wish for but none of those
precipitous mountains and gradients to be found in
some counties. It is endlessly diverse in its scenery,
embracing windswept heath, long beaches of sand or
shingle, cliffs, extensive woods, gently undulating
countryside, lakes, and above all historic towns
of a range and quality that cannot fail to
be impressive. Norwich of course is everyone's ideal
of a county centre; then there are ports and resorts,
market and industrial towns, tourist centres
and backwater settlements. Norfolk is also a big
county, and it takes you a long time to realise that
you have a long way to travel tround it to see everything -
even if you could ! But beware: the county can cast
a spell over the visitor that makes him or her
wish to return year after year, and sometimes for good.

        If you look on your map of East Anglia, Great
Yarmouth sits on the coast only marginally not as far
east as Lowestoft, and on the wide river Waveney which
strangely detours away from Lowestoft and heads north
to provide splendid water services for Yarmouth.
The rivers Yare and Bure converge on the town to add
to its water sources and port facilities, and the town
has anciently been one of the most important of the
region and county.

        Yarmouth was a town and port in the 12th
century, and interestingly its face was to the riverside
and not the sea until the 19th century. The shape of the
place is also strange, long and thin, and originally with
later 13th and early 14th century walls   23 feet high
with 16 towers and 10 gates - a very substantial medieval
effort, though not much more than a mile in length
because the river protected the longest side. What
remains are substantial amounts of walling plus the Rows,
the remnant of alleyways which linked the several main
streets and upto c1940 made the town most fascinating to
peruse on foot.

        The town into the 18th century had a large
port business and considerable fishing fleet to bring
in wealth, and this shows in the medieval churches of the
time.

Carmelite and Franciscan friaries were in the town in the 1220s, which is very early and shows the importance of the town. The latter have left some ruins though Queen Street covers most of them, whilst the former have left nothing at all. Then there were Dominicans established in the 1260s, but thanks to a fire of 1525 not a thing remains of the church, and thanks to the Dissolution nothing of the rest of the complex. At Gorleston , just over the river, was a house of Austin friars of some importance and with a notable library: the remaining buildings collapsed in the early 19th century.

The town's St Nicholas of course is the star of the district, arguably the largest parish church of Britain, at some 23,000 square feet - truly vast. It was attached to a small Benedictine priory or cell based on Norwich, and the first church was of c1100, which is very early indeed. It was enlarged in the 13th and 14th century, allowed to fall into disrepair in the 17th and 18th centuries, extensively restored last century and then again after the last war to produce an epic parish building.

Plenty of other churches grace the town, including Dissenting ones and a c1714 parish church. Then there are public buildings - town hall, schools, c1810 hospital, several quays, toll and customs houses, and mostly of the 19th and 20th centuries. What happened in the town's history was that it became a reasonably fashionable resort in the later 18th century, but this changed when with the arrival of the railway in the mid 19th century in came daytrippers and others of the lower echelons of society ! The ensuing new seaside resort of the Victorian years was not a place for the elite of society !

The resort spread straight north along the coast and away from old Yarmouth. The result is that you can enjoy a popular seaside resort with all that it means, and then step back to savour the sights and smells of the port and quays, and explore the remaining network of the Rows and other parts of the old quarter - museums, medieval timber framed properties, Georgian merchant houses and premises, in considerable numbers. So do wander down South and Hall Quays, the Market Place , Church Plain, St George's Plain, the Rows, King Street and other places for it really is a pleasant urban environment without most of the smells which would have been associated even last century with a herring and commercial port !

EAST DEREHAM

There are two Derehams some miles apart, and
of widely differing character and size. West Dereham
is best known for its fine Norman parish church and
for its bits and pieces of the ruins of the Premonstratensian abbey founded in 1188 for the canons of that order
and possessor of land and property in 33 Norfolk
parishes. It was one of the richest and most important
of the order's houses, and when Bishop Redman - who
was abbot of Shap in Cumbria as well as bishop and
holder of all sorts of honours and posts - repeatedly
visited the house here it was in excellent condition.
What a pity nothing remains.

East Dereham is the market town rather than
village, as is its twin.   I first came to know the town
through its literary connections: George Borrow, whose
enormous, interesting but heavyweight books I once had
to read, was early on raised here since his parents
(in 1793) were farm tenants (but was he born here or
at his gran's house ?) . And the ill and depressed
poet William Cowper died here in 1800 after being
brought for several years to a house in the town by
his friends.

The Market Place displays numbers of
Georgian houses which suggests strongly the wealth of the
farming community whose money encouraged such buildings
by professional and merchant families. Assembly rooms of
the 1750s shows the main place of entertainment for
those minor gentry and similar families who sought
town life at cheap rates (Bath and London being far too
dear of course !) and took town houses for the season.
Corn exchange of the   Victorian era dislays the
continued prosperity of farming in spite of rural
problems.

Lots of town inns and pubs from the later medieval
and 17th and 18th centuries: old cottages, brick of
various colours, timber framing and pargetting . 18th
century guildhall, several Dissenting churches,
and the type of streets with the sorts of buildings
that most well off towns have had at one time make
this an especially attractive place of resort either to
live or to visit, and I suspect tourism is one of the
boom industries too.

The parish church of   St Nicholas
is a mighty effort in the most proud and prominent
setting, complete with great crossing tower and
detached bell tower: lots of those fascinating things
which make a church so interesting inside are here in
numbers - glass, monuments, furnishings and the like
which will detail you for an hour or two.

The church was Norman but regularly extended
or rebuilt or improved over the mdidle ages and in
later centuries to make a remarkable edifice of
grand proportions.

KINGS LYNN

One of the urban successes of the centuries is Kings Lynn, for it epitomises all that is best and most valued about country towns: picturesque setting by the river and great stretches of open land, fine churches and public buildings, scores of well built, historic houses and businesses of many and varied architectural styles, sufficient work to make the town economically prosperous for generation after generation of local folk, and all those cherished historical places with which to attract in tourists as bonus. Funnily enough you remember the two great market places above all else, for there is the Saturday Market with its church of St Margaret, and the smaller but still large Tuesday Market with its church of St Nicholas.

The former market place is the older, and it seems ironic in view of later centuries that the Tuesday market was called "new" for centuries even though itself dating from the mid 12th century, Norman venture of the bishop.

St Margaret's is big, somewhere around 235 feet long and with two towers, a Norman church that was rebuilt larger in the 13th century and much remodelled and altered in successive generations. St Nicholas was simply a chapel of ease, and is all c1410 apart from a tower of several centuries earlier and itself a replacement for the Norman chapel. Quite dissimilar to St Margaret, which is a good thing really since two giants would lead to rivalry ! The town also has a number of other churches, including Red Mount chapel, a c1490 building used mainly by the pilgrims on the way to Walsingham and relieving them of their money as well as their prayers !

The town sits on the river Great Ouse which offered the middle ages the main supply port for the entire region. The wealth attracted the friars, and in Lynn there were a remarkable 5 houses. The friars of the Sack was abolished in the 1270s though members did live on into the next century; the Franciscans have left their brilliant octagonal steeple of the church but not much else, though at one time there were about 40 friars (plus all their workers). The Dominicans have left nothing, but the Carmelites   left behind their brick gateway (and of course their stones were reused in other properties after 1540).   And the Austin house has just its one arch surviving. These were all large and prosperous houses, so their destruction must have had a dramatic effect on town life.

The Benedictine priory in the town has an interesting story behind it: the bishop of Norwich at that date was the powerful Herbert de Losinga, who had, against all laws, bought his See, and in atonement was forced to found this monastery and church (with others in the diocese). It was thus both parish church and monastic one, and its chancel survives along with the monastic quarters partly rebuilt into a house.

The town has however far more than a list of medieval churches and monastic histories. It has a splendid set of historic civic buildings - gaol of the 1780s, flint and stone guildhall of the early 15th century, assembly rooms of the 1760s, town hall in sympathetic style of the 1890s. Corn exchange, courts and so on grace the town, but the star of this ensemble is the customs house of the 1680s, a brilliant essay in Doric and Ionic style with hipped roof, dormers, lantern, arched and once open ground floor.

If you wisely explore on foot then it is the two
market places which offer the shops and businesses, and
a spaciousness usually absent in old towns which tended to
be jam packed with medieval life. Enjoy their happy
jumble of various architectural styles and building
materials, colours and decorations; do not miss the
riverside district too, though it is not that attractive
and was ever devoted to commerce. King Street and
Priory Lane, High Street and Bridge Street, Southgate
Street and Norfolk Street, plus others, offer a sense of
timeless and historic urban life which is only found
in the rest of the county in Norwich. Brick and flint,
classical decoration and medieval restraint, stone and
timber framed and jettied buildings, all are there
for the tourist to enjoy.

THETFORD

When working on the history of East Anglia I
was taken aback by the ancient importance of Thetford,
set deep in the south of Norfolk right against the
Suffolk boundary. It was the seat of the Anglo-
Saxon kings of East Anglia and was a stronghold and
burgh by the time that the 7th century bishopric was
removed from little North Elmham to much larger
Thetford in the 10thcentury. In line with their policy
of moving Sees to the largest towns of a region, the
Normans removed the cathedral and bishopric to Norwich
in 1095, but Thetford retained considerable regional
importance throughout the middle ages.

On sign of wealth and economic success
was the religious houses. Thetford was distinguished by
the wealth and diversity of its Orders, with an early
priory of Cluniac monks established in 1103 by Roger
Bigod. This house enjoyed rich lands and wool income,
and was lucky in having many relics of saints which
brought in the pilgrims and money. It was also the
burial place for a number of Howards including dukes of
Norfolk. Today the foundations are exposed of what was
a major monastic settlement , and the prior's house
plus substantial amounts of walling also exists to be
examined by the curious. The Benedictine priory of
about 1020 for monks only lasted till c1160, when it
was abandoned to Benedictine nuns from the house at

Ling and Bury St Edmunds. It seems to have been one of the best regulated of houses but was never big or rich. The church, interestingly, was made into a secular barn ! This still exists along with other bits and pieces.

William de Warenne, earl of Surrey, founded a house of Augustinian canons in 1139 which was situated on the Suffolk side of the river Thet. Sadly its surviving buildings form farm accommodation, and there is not really much to see. The Dominican friary has left parts of the church in a modern school: their church was the old cathedral of the diocese of Thetford, and again its loss is a sad one for it would have been a Saxon church of national importance. Another friary, this time of Austin friars, dates from 1389 (very late indeed) but it was a much smaller and poorer house than that of its strong, rival Dominicans.

The town does also have literary connections in that Tom Paine, notorious author of THE RIGHTS OF MAN, was born here in 1737 and worked for his father for a time before America beckoned this restless, combattive man. His advocacy of democracy and freedom upset the authorities too much, and he lived in various countries and towns. There used to be a Tom Paine society in the town, and perhaps still is.

Thetford, as might be imagined, did rather badly out of the Dissolution of the monasteries in the 1530s and thereafter was a much sleepier place for centuries. There was an interesting but failed attempt to make it a spa about 1820, but it came to little.   The town has the benefit of many grey brick, flint and timber framed properties of varying sizes and dates, and in general its old buildings have been better preserved than in many towns.

Three old churches still grace the town, as might be expected, and there is a guildhall but this is a rebuilding job of 1900. The castle is just earthworks of the motte and bailey kind of the early Norman days, with the emphasis moving to Norwich and its grander castle. The Market Place King Street, Bridge Street, Castle Street and White Hart Street are some of the main

thoroughfares and all display many old inns and pubs, business premises and houses with dates from the later medieval decades into the early 19th century, with not too much that might be construed as jarring from the Victorian or mdoern years. Overall, my impression was of a very hospitable place both for residents and tourists with enough local industrial development to keep it prosperous and tourism not too rampant - yet !

WYMONDHAM

Not far out of Norwich, to the south east and on
the road to London, is Wymondham, but instead of having
lived in the shadow of its great neighbour, this
town has for centuries enjoyed considerable wealth
thanks to wool, cloth, to the great medieval abbey,
and these days to various small scale businesses which
find it more convenient than Norwich, and to many
residents who get fed up battling with city traffic
and prefer the quieter life in a town where you
can still park more or less where you want.

The Benedictine abbey of St Mary and St
Alban was founded in 1107 by William de Albini,
later earl of Arundel and a powerful Norman figure.
First as a priory the house was under the control
of St Albans, and after 300 years of seemingly constant
disputes between the two sets of monks and officials,
Wymondham became an abbey in 1449 - which meant
independence. The priory-abbey also endured constant
conflict with the town: the founder had intended that
the great new church should serve both the monks
and the parish, but constant rows led to each building
their own tower, a solid stone wall between the two
halves, and the present weird looking fabric. Much of
the fabric stands - the nave and one aisle of the abbey
church is beautifully roofed over, but most of the
monastic buildings have gone.

Silly isn't it that such rows should ruin
things ? Still the town showed an admirable independence
from so wealthy a house and presumably did not live in
its shadow !

One of those major fires which were constant
risks to towns in the past centuries happened in
Wymondham in 1615 and most of the old timber framed
place went down to ashes. Thus the abbey has nothing
much in the way of serious architectural rivals,
but at least rebuilding in the 17th century led to
some nice houses and premises, and the 18th century
brought new Georgian style and details.

The Market Place is the centre and displays
a most attractive market cross of 1617, octagonal
and open on the ground floor. I suppose that if you
would like old inns the 17th century Green Dragon,
Crossed Keys and Kings Head will offer hospitality and
visual pleasure !

Georgian houses look to be best represented
in the Market Place district and Middleton Street,
especially Caius House and others in delightful hand
made red bricks - just compare them with the odd
house of brutal, coarse, inelegant machine made
bricks. The severe side of local life is seen in the
Bridewell or gaol, Classical Georgian of 1787
and for a brutal purpose.

It was good to see the chapel of St Thomas a
Beckett, apparently a late 12th century, Norman,
church put up to the saint's memory: still very
Norman today though with later work to the fabric.

The railway snakes to the south of the town
and in the 19th century brought in many new people,
new jobs, new wealth, residents and religious
diversity to this little town. Do have a look if
you can, at the various villages and their parish
churches, cottages, manor houses and so on: their
names are a fascinating study in themselves !
Spooner Row, Morley St Botolph, Wicklewood and
so many others with the customary tangle of minor
roads and lanes even so close to Norwich. Just up

the road and you are into Norwich where things
seem rather different and the pace of life so much
quicker - though to no advantage.

NORWICH

         Norwich is one of the major cities of Europe,
and if you visit the city for more than a few hours
you will see why I make this claim.   Already in Saxon
times it was a commercial centre for the entire region,
having grown up where the river Wensum bends back
on itself and meets a colleague, and to this importance
the Normans added the great cathedral priory. For the
next 400 years Norwich was really only second to London
in urban importance, though rivalled by York and at
times Bristol, and the enormous merchant wealth of the
place can be gauged from the many medieval churches (of
which there were over 50) plus religious houses whose
precincts rivalled the premises and houses of the
trading classes.   Wool, cloth and trade ruled, and after
the Dissolution of the c1540 years the town retained its
regional lead though during the 19th century the rise of
enormous industrial towns in the midlands and north of
England meant as a population centre it became third rank.
Industrial growth did occur but on a modest scale: even
so a town which had over 5,000 residents in the late 14th
century, 30,000 c1700, and 40,000 c1800 was very
substantial.

         The city broke out of its medieval walls only
in the Victorian years, and from then on the place has
combined its historic roles with the modern needs of
industry, business and housing estates.

In literary circles it was no surprise that talent migrated to Norwich through the centuries. Anna Sewell wrote BLACK BEAUTY at her mum's home in Catton in the Victorian years - her mother being the well known author of children's books, Mary Sewell. George Borrow was raised and educated in the town in the early 19th century, articled to a lawyer, and gleaned much of his material for such books as ROMANY RYE, LAVENGRO etc from his experiences in the city with the locals and the gypsies.

Such a rich city encouraged Dissent of every shade in politics and religion: readers will know of the wide circle of intellectual and educated women and men in the city from the 1770s through to the 1850s, often centred on the Unitarian and Quaker places of worship. Thus Harriet Martineau, who in later years tried to bring Cumbrian workers into the 19th century (!) spent her youth and early career here (and her family produced other brilliant writers too); the Gurneys and the Opies were part of that culturally advanced grouping.

In earlier times it comes as no surprise to find that the Pastons owned considerable property in Norwich in the middle ages. The Elizabethan dramatist Robert Green was born and educated in Norwich; and it was de rigueur that the literary and artistic set should place Norwich on their annual itinerary (at least when they were young) - thus men like Southey found congenial company before his days as poet laureate.

Religiously the city was the centre for East Anglia for centuries.

The cathedral priory was founded by Herbert de Losinga, one of those ruthless and able men thrown up by county society who became enormously influential. He founded the pair in 1096 and the two became of unrivalled influence in the city's affairs - which led to substantial difficulties with townsfolk who wished for less interference in their city affairs !

There were two small dependent Benedictine cells for monks in the city too, plus one for Benedictine nuns known as Carrow priory and often needing the aid of the bishop in dealing with difficult tenants of their many lands - the convent received many gifts from county families whose daughters entered the establishment. Remains of the nunnery are still to be seen .

Friars headed for Norwich in exceptional numbers so that there were 6 friaries in late 13th century times involving scores of friars and much wealth. The main remains belong to the Dominicans, whose church is the only one in the country to remain as an entity.

After the Dissolution the town became focal point for Dissent, and there were exceptionally influential congregations of Quakers, Unitarians and most of the other major denominations from the 17th into the present century.

The first Norman cathedral was of c1100 and took generations to complete: its ground plan is famous as being the only Norman one to have survived the centuries. What impresses you about the cathedral is the tower and spire at well over 300 feet, so that in so low lying a setting this feature redeems the view. It is secluded too, with an enormous area of close and precincts attached. So it is a Norman fabric but with many later changes of detail and emphasis: absolutely splendid rooves of the 15th century, rebuilt spire, new buttresses and clerestorey of the later medieval years, and 14th century cloisters.

It possesses one of those radiating east ends which were usual on the continent - the Chevet - but rare here, and comparable to Gloucester's. The interior furnishings are so extensive that they require a book in themselves, and you should spend the day perusing and examining the paintings, glass, sculpture, woodwork, masonry, and the rest.

Enjoy too the ruins of the bishop's palace, the old deanery, the gates, the many houses, all of medieval to early 19th century dates and a superb array of architectural details - though the bishop's palace of the Victorian years jars the senses, and one could wish for one as at Wells.

More than 30 of the medieval parish churches have come down in various amounts of masonry, so that over 20 have been lost, but you need a few days to explore the riches offered by these buildings in what was the finest array of medieval architecture in the country outside London: and still quite stunning despite the fabrics often having other uses today as so many are not needed.

The city's Colegate Congregational chapel or Old Meeting, the illustrious Octagon of Unitarian fame, the Gildencroft Quaker meeting, are all historic places of whole communities of people set apart by their beliefs from the Established Church.

If you wish to see a fine museum go to the castle, which is more or less an enormous Norman keep 90 by 90 by 70 feet, on a hill, with earthworks but not much in the way of other old stonework, and now the splendid county museum. Anthony Salvin was brought in to repair etc in the 1830s but few have been happy with his efforts on what had been the county gaol !

The old town walls still exist in part, second only to London in length and height, and you can still enjoy a walk round them now - but do not expect a Chester or York experience !

A notable array of public buildings continues with the shire hall of the 1820s, the 15th and 16th century Guildhall, a grim but imposing city hall of the 1930s, and the superb assembly rooms of the very best Georgian of the 1750s. The list could go on: several other museums and displays in ancient buildings, including the medieval and later bridewell, the socalled Great Hospital, medieval and later and very

impressive, and a whole district such as Elm Hill made up of the sort of houses any town would be proud to have by themselves, with here a whole street of them (district in fact !).

The town of course is not just its wealth of historic buildings and streets, but they do make a place so much nicer ! If you have the time do get the relevant map and details and walk round what was the old city (into last century) and you can easily see where it ends from the walls, old buildings and the enormous number of new ones which suddenly went up outside the walls. The city is a very large administrative centre- thousandsare employed in the offices of local and national firms and the advice first given to me was to avoid the rush hour. Our first two trips to view the town, 20 years ago, were on Sundays so as to avoid the crush, and thanks to the boom years of the 1980s the traffic is even worse now. An acquaintances tell me that Norwich continues to be notorious for its jams and crush !

Norwich remains a dynamic place - just look at the success of homegrown industries and of such establishments as the university of East Anglia for example - and highly prized by residents (despite the traffic !) and tourists. I suppose if you could choose something to remember, not on the grand scale of the cathedral or castle, you might recall the Old Music House in King Street, at one time a 12th century town residence of one of the many Jews who lived in the town.

Interestingly, the town, like York and London, had a whole Jewish community - one wonders if they were treated any better here in Norwich ! Migrants continue to pour into town, whether from London or abroad - the district has gone through one of the highest of all the nation's property rises in the last 10 years. The medieval and later Flemish migrants brought their talents for cloth making and other trades too, and it is still true that Norwich benefits tremendously from its influx of outsiders. It so dominates East Anglia that when you look

on your modern maps, all the roads seem to converge on
and radiate from Norwich: a sort of wheel of
communications for thousands of square miles.

DISS

    Diss is right on the Suffolk border in the
south of Norfolk and is best known for its mere
and park. It is picturesque thanks to a jumble of
architectural styles ranging from medieval through to
pleasant Victorian, and the Market Place is the best
district for showing of this. The Dolphin inn is
half timbered with gables and jettied upper storeys;
the Shambles is mostly Victorian , and there are a
number of older fabrics sheltering behind more
fashionable later facades. Overlooking the three sided
Market Place is St Mary's, a medieval church with a
tower of the c1300 era , a Victorian chancel and
old masonry elsewhere . The old ritual demanded
processional activity, and arches on the base of the
tower in most unusual (today) fashion illustrate
this need. Inside are all the usual bits and pieces of
church furnishings which so interest the tourist
and visitor.

    Such a town as Diss offers both locals and
tourists a great deal: it also evidently offered
the residents of other centuries much, for there is an
unusual religious diversity which is not often
found in the district. So as well as Church of England
you could have attended Quakers, Baptists, Methodists,
Congregational and Unitarian church services last
century ! It suggests too the political activity of the

town in last century was extreme ! Just to the north
is Burston, scene for many years earlier this century of
the famous school rebellion, when the large village
followed its schoolteachers into their own school
after a quarrel with the local clergy - readers may
well know that religious and political difficulties in
the county have been common, and that such organisations
as the farmworkers unions have had an interesting time !

On a gentler note, Diss was the living of the
medieval poet John Skelton, a real Cambridge brain,
but also a cleric (here from the 1490s till his death
in 1529) and writer of what were classics of the day.

SWAFFHAM

Recently I watched a programme on Edwin and
Willa Muir, those two literary characters of some
recent fame, who lived in Swaffham in their later years
and produced some famous books and translations of books
such as those by Franz Kafka, all from their cottage in
Swaffham. Swaffham is an attractive market town,
now thankfully enjoying new life after the opening of
a bypass to relieve congestion, but the town is still
at the hub of all the lanes and roads of the district.

The parish church is one of the biggest in
the district and set almost secretly away from but close
to the town centre. The impressive tower is of the
1500s, the main body of the church of 30 to 60
years earlier, and tied up with the story of the Pedlar
of Swaffham who is supposed to have paid for the
aisle of the church to be built out of the treasure he
discovered in a dream. A good deal of things to see
both inside and outside the church too.

The town centre has the usual Market Place
and this time with an elegant Market Cross of the 1780s,
paid for and commissioned by the earl of Oxford -
it even has a figure of Ceres, the god of corn etc,
on the lead covered, domed roof. The town has its old

corn exchange, a very urban facility serving the rural
hinterland. It also possesses a shire hall, of all
things, which is a bit cheeky too ! There are assembly
rooms, a number of old pubs and inns, various timber
framed and brick properties, no lack of Georgian
houses and business premises, and particular emphasis
on the architecture of c1780 - c1840, the times of
high corn and farm incomes which encouraged such
provincial culture. It was the peak of all county towns
too, still without the Londonising nature of railways
and the like.

BURNHAM MARKET   and BURNHAM OVERY

        The Burnhams, as they have become known,
comprise an original seven parishes in the north of the
county not far inland from the sea. The proximity of
so many large villages or small towns says much for the
medieval wealth of the county based on wool and cloth and
farming, and in some ways this has continued to this
day in this very attractive district.

        Burnham Market possesses one of those fine
main streets with a blend of cottages and grander
houses as well as inns and businesses, with not much in
the way of modern intrusions , with at one end the excellent
medieval parish church of St Mary and behind that one of
Sir John Soane's architectural masterpieces, 1780s
Westgate Hall (I think the village was known as that,
Westgate, for some time).

        Burnham Overy displays its two windmills
(which are quite dissimilar) and a Norman parish church
with central tower. Overy and Market are the two
largest of the group of Burnhams.

        Horatio Nelson was born in the parsonage at
Burnham Thorpe in 1758, and his illustrious career in
the navy needs no comment: I always wonder if these
men kept any local accent when they became famous ?

People find the parish church at Thorpe very rewarding
with its monuments by the very best of sculptors -
Lough and Flaxman for instance.   Burnham Norton had
a Carmelite friary from the 1250s founded by Sir Ralph
de Hemenhale and Sir William de Calthorp - a fair amount
of the old friary remains to be viewed including a gate
house, walling and work in a house. It produced some
interesting friars including learned ones, several
executed or tried for treason and the like. The other
Burnhams are distinguished by their churches and
their attractive but modest cottages and houses - a unique
regional grouping.

CAISTER ON SEA

        Caister on Sea is only separated these days from
its far larger neighbour, Great Yarmouth, by a golf
course and odd bits of green. It lies on that splendid
Norfolk coast facing east and Europe, and has one of the
largest of excavated Roman towns at about 30 acres.
Cobbled roads, the usual main buildings, flint walls
10 feet thick, and all the refuse one would associate
with a Roman town have been found; interestingly
it is on the exposed coast for pirates and invasion,
and scores of Saxon graves have been found nearby.

        The settlement of Caister is more or less a
suburb, but it was once quite distinct from Yarmouth.
The castle is of brick and has a moat, and there are
remains of various gates, curtain walling, towers and
other buildings within the moat. One corner of the large
site covered by the former castle complex is given
over to the Georgian looking hall. As many will
know, this was the home of the Paston family - the
letters of John and Margaret Paston have become
important sources of information for the 15th century
and have been published.

        The main parish church of the town is Holy
Trinity, which is a 13th century and later fabric
with a good deal to interest visitors despite later

alterations. I should think that the font of this
church, which happens to be over 5 feet by 3 feet
in girth, ranks as one of the largest of the region !

HARLESTON

        Harleston sits right by the Suffolk border
and on the river Waveney, at the centre of a whole
complex of roads and byways which deserve exploring,
and of villages and parishes which demand attention.
It has the distinction of both and old and a new
Market Place, too. Unfortunately the town's main
church is an undistinguished one of the 1870s -
St John the Baptist.

        The old Market Place shows off an array of
nice town houses from the later 17th to early 19th
centuries, in both stone and brick, and is far superior
from an architectural point of view than anything else
in the town. In the new Market Place the quality
of the environment is strangely worse, and lots of
Victorian and modern development has taken over.

        The best old inn I suppose must be the
Swan, which combines restoration masonry with that of the
18th century when business involving coaching was
burgeoning forth and bringing in ample revenue to
encourage rebuilding on a larger scale: thus an older
wing vies with a larger, bolder Georgian front - very
good to see. Lots of enjoyable properties grace various
streets of Harleston, but the best is reckoned to be
Candler's House, described as earliest Georgian, and with

a high hipped roof, interesting decorative features
including segmental pediment, and much more.

ACLE

      Acle is on the main roads which meet on the way
between Yarmouth and the coast, and Norwich, and the
accompanying Z bends need watching if you are the
driver. The settlement grew up round the door of the
Augustinian priory of Weybridge founded in 1225 by
Roger Bigod, earl of Norfolk, and prominent force in
the county. In fact it is one of the most mysterious of
regional monasteries since little is known of its
history even so far as to disputes and rows: it owned
various advowsons (right of presentation to a parish
living) and a fair amount of property however. You might
know that not a thing remains of its buildings !
An inn is on the site today and is supposed to have parts
of the old medieval masonry attached. The little town
(or large village !) of Acle has a number of those
pleasant terraces of cottages and some larger, Georgian
and classically embellished properties too. The star
of the place must be the parish church, St Edmund's,
which displays a strange round tower of the 13th
century. It displays much else too including Norman
work, a rare type of font, and enough to keep the
tourist interested for an hour.

REEPHAM

The map shows Reepham to be at the centre of
a tangle of minor roads, the sort you need to explore
on foot or by bicycle, and to the south of the
town is the famous Norfolk Wildlife Park and its
fascinating collection of animals.

Known to historians for its unique (?)
show of three churches sharing one churchyard Reepham
has many of those modest little 18th and 19th century
cottages and a number of Georgian town houses which are
still nice to see even if they are common to so many
East Anglian market towns. The Market Place remains the
town's centre, and it is nice to see a small market town
still more or less as it was a century and more ago.
Of the old pubs and inns, the Kings Arms is perhaps
the nicest, and of the houses it is Dial House, the
sort of c1700 property put up by wealthy professional
and business men of the region.

The three churches include the ruined Hackford
church, a medieval fabric which was mostly destroyed in
the 1540s. By one of those curious quirks of history
the parish church of Whitwell is in Reepham's churchyard,
that is St Michael's, an overrestored building but
with the glory of a big late medieval tower. Next door
is Reepham's parish church, St Mary, again medieval
and far too attended to in the 19th century to make it
one of the notable ones of the county. It does have
a better interior, with impressive monuments and brasses,
woodwork and stonework.

EAST HARLING

The church is of the lae 13th, 14th and
15th centuries, a happy compilation of the best from
each style. Just look at the stalls, screens,
glass, stone monuments, all impressive and speaking of
some lavish craftsmanship and expense over the
generations.

It is hard to omit from this book many of those
large villages which have much of the small town about
them, and east Harling is a case in point so I include
it here, however briefly. This is flattest Norfolk
not far from Thetford and the river Thet and its
marshland area, and just north of the Suffolk border.
The medieval manor house and the Lovell family who
occupied it have gone: the Lovells of course were at
their height in the late 15th and early 16th century
as they rubbed shoulders with the royals and eminent
nobles c1485, but seem to have lost a lot including
their lives for dallyings with revolt in the time of
Henry VII - witness their ruined Minster Lovell over
in Oxfordshire. The settlement retains a number of
rows of good properties of varying size but of a
conformity in quality. The star of the place, as is so
often the case when the big house has gone from a
small centre, is the parish church.

The church of St Peter and St Paul is one of the
county's most spectacular from any point of view,
with a high tower surrounded with buttresses and
with a miniature spire rising like some sort of fountain
of the c1300 style. Inside it is the impressive hammerbeam
roof that you remember, a great show of complexity in
woodcrafting which is too often under-rated against
stone masonry.

WATTON

impressive: again with the Norman round tower and an
unspoiled c1300 body to it . Inside there is excellent
medieval masonry, plus lots of monuments, glass,
woodwork and similar elements which go to make up
an interesting church.

        Another tiny town is Watton, lying on the
A1075 road between Thetford and East Dereham and easily
overlooked by every traveller even today. The town
centre as such is the High Street and its roads
surrounding, and there is a clock tower to replace the
old market cross, of the restoration period, and with
lock ups for naughty people and complete with cupola
and weathervane: very urban and villagey at once.
The church of St Mary has one of those Norman round
towers and a sadly badly treated 13th century body:
interest remains, but it is by no means an outstanding
fabric.

        The nearby village of Merton figures in
literary history because it was the place visited by
Edward Fitzgerald - whose stamping ground was usually
the Suffolk coast and Woodbridge district nearby -
who is best known for his translations of the poems of
Omar Khyamm which attracted attention in Victorian
times. Fitzgerald had a great pal in the vicar of
Merton, George Crabbe (a familiar name to historians
because his grandfather was the poet Crabbe);
oddly enough Fitzgerald died in the parsonage during
his visit to Crabbe in 1883.

        Merton's church is reasonably

ATTLEBOROUGH

Another of those small rural towns dependent on
the prosperity of farming for many centuries is
Attleborough, astride the main road from Thetford to
Norwich, and given a boost last century in the midst
of rural decline by the railway. A big village in
many ways, but how can somewherethat used to have a
Corn Exchange be anything but a town ! The manor
house or hall for the town is a 17th century timber
framed property with a moat which looks remarkably
large for so modest a place: the town has a number of
17th and 18th century properties of varying shapes and
sizes, and some buildings have medieval origins but
newer facades as modern fashions demanded and
greater wealth encouraged and allowed.

The parish church used to have a Norman chancel
and apsidal east end, but these have gone but a Norman
central tower and much Norman masonry remains. Most of
the building has the air of the 14th century decorated
style, and a college of priests in the mid 14th
century led to more spending on certain aspects of the
church. Plenty of interest inside too in the medieval
wall paintings of a type once very common and now
quite scarce, in the stained glass, the stalls and
pulpit, the misericords and so on. The star of the interior
however is the Rood screen, a very substantial work of the

later medieval years with a number of fine decorative
works including painted figures and panels, and the sort
of thing that other churches would like to possess - most
screens of this sort went in the 16th century Reformation
and were rarely retained or rebuilt.

Halfway to Diss is Kenninghall, with its
excellent Norman and later parish church, and the
ruins of the former mansion of the dukes of Norfolk,
built in early Tudor times when the family were exceptionally
powerful. Their intrigues led to their downfall,
and the duke was only saved by the death of Henry VIII
in 1547 - but his son Henry Howard, early of Surrey, and
a brilliant young courtier with considerable intellectual
abilities (including poetry) had already lost his head
on the block. Henry had lived here at this ruin in
its days of glory.

HUNSTANTON

smaller resort, and a lovely stretch of coastline.

To the south is the settlement of Heacham
and the marvellous display of every possible shade of
lavender at the Norfolk lavender centre - a brilliant
profusion of blues when it all flowers, with nothing
quite like the ocean of blue flowers of magnificent
pefumes in any part of the country.

Hunstanton is the only Norfolk town and resort
on the great expanse of the Wash, and it faces, uniquely,
west. Endless shingle and sand faces you at this resort
which has both old and new towns: the old quarter is centred
on the mansion of the Lestrange family, a big moated place
which combines late medieval with styles of the early 17th
and 19th centuries. The old parish church of St Mary
was drastically restored in the 1850s, and its fabric
spoiled: there remains a fair amount to see including
the remnants of 13th and 14th century masonry, the
Lestrange and other brasses, and a very late medieval
screen of size.

The new resort was purposely developed by the
manor house owners, the Lestranges, in the 1860s and 1870s.
The main opportunity came with the railway in 1862 and
this opened new ideas of mass tourism to the place and
the subsequent lucrative development of a new quarter
and town including pier and promenade. Having seen so
many historic towns of the county I felt let down here,
for this is an excellent example of reasonably boring
and certainly tedious Victorian building, street after
street of it in brick - and harsh, machine made brick
too often.

Still there are the views, endless choice of
hotels and guesthouses, all that one would want in a

FAKENHAM

Fakenham is now bypassed by the main roads
which lead all over the county , where once it was something
of a crossroads and had a clutch of coaching inns and
all that the passengers required for their wearisome
journeys. The Market Place, the Square and the surrounding
district need to be seen on foot to appreciate what
a pleasant little urban centre it is, and the parish
church of St Peter and St Paul displays a very fine
tower which is something of a landmark. It has lots to
show off to the tourists who decides to turn off into the
town and to walk to the church. Not far out of Fakenham
are many of the typical English villages which so catch
the imagination - the Ryburghs, the Snorins, both with a
Great and a Little, and the superbly named Swanton Novers.

A few miles to the north are the Walsinghams,
next door to each other, and they remain places of
pilgrimage dating from 1061 when Lady Richeld had her
vision and built a shrine that became one of the most visited
in the nation. The socalled Slipper Chapel was established
a mile out at Houghton St Giles so pilgrims could take off
their shoes and walk the last mile barefoot !

A house of Augustinian canons was founded in the
1150s and in some way got control of the shrine to Mary
so that thereafter, into the 1530s, the canons enjoyed
an extremely high income from the pilgrims. The priory

was one of the richest in the region thanks to this
income, and today you can admire what substantial ruins
are left of this, the richest house of Norfolk after
the Norwich one.

There was too a house of Franciscan friars
just 200 yards from the parish church of Little
Walsingham, founded just before the great plague of
1348, and as one might expect, bitterly opposed by the
Austin canons up the road ! The two parish churches of
the villages are also quite magnificent thanks to wealth
brought in during the middle ages by pilgrims.

Each village has its set of attractive houses and
cottages too, and today a stream of pilgrims continue to
come rather as they do on Lindisfarne. The cult of the
Virgin Mary was revived in the 1890s and a new shrine
built in the 1930s: the several ruins, shrines, churches
and the like form a quite exceptional group in the
region, and when I was there were attracting enormous
numbers in.

NORTH WALSHAM

alterations last century. Inside there is a reasonable
amount to see in the way of furnishings - screens, woodwork
and monuments for instance.

Down the road to the south of the town those who
enjoyed BLACK BEAUTY in all its many manifestations
on screen, TV and in books will know that Anna Sewell
knew this area well. She had learned about horses on her
grandparents' farm, Dudwick House in Buxton, as a child,
and her famous book of 1877 (she died the next year,
only in her 50s) placed this property and the surrounding
countryside in it. Up the road at Lamas she was buried
the following year.

My Sheringham friend used to take the bus in the
1960s early each morning for the ride to North Walsham's
grammar school : it always seemed to me a long way to have
to go, but then the county demands long journeys by its
great size. The market place, Church Street, Aylsham
Road, Mundesley Street and Bacton Road show off the sort of
modest houses and properties to be seen in so many
unassuming, moderately prosperous little towns. Of note
is the market cross, an early 17th century one of timber
and octagonal, lit by a double lantern. Odd classical
Georgian houses rub shoulders with coaching inns.
Such towns usually have those old gardens which are so
characteristic of the best townscapes, and North
Walsham is no exception with enough on display to interest
the horticulturally minded tourists.

The parish church is big and has a rough looking
tower which was never rebuilt adequately after one of those
collapses so typical of the 18th century. The tower used
to be about 150 feet, which made it one of the noblest
in the region (and without a spire too); the church
is slightly longer than that, so the proportions were
just right.

The church is broadly medieval, and especially of
the 14th and 15th centuries in spite of considerable

AYLSHAM

Aylsham lies at the crossroads of what seem
to be a dozen minor byways not that far north of
Norwich. I first came to know the place due to
associations with the most famous gardener of his
generation, Humphrey Repton,   who is buried in the
churchyard and who had lived locally for some time.
After marrying Repton was often away on business but
his home was at Sustead Hall just out of town, and
his relatives seem to have been thick on the ground in
the district. The parish church is one of the county's
finest, basically 14th century inside but with
a magnificent porch of the 15th century, and exterior
generally of that time and style. There is a west gallery,
stained glass and wealth of monuments including ones to
Repton and his relatives; fine reredos, screen and pulpit
too and much to detain the visitor.

The streets radiate off the Market Place and
the little town is known for its red brick Georgian
properties which speak of some affluence in the 18th
and early 19th century, perhaps from farming rents,
tithes and professional fees. Aylsham Old Hall, of the
1680s, the manor house of the 1600s, the Knoll of
about 1700, speak of quality and pride; Millgate Street,
Red Lion Street and White Hart Street provide classical
18th century properties.

Out of town is Blickling Hall, one of the
nation's major Jacobean properties, a brick house put
up in the years 1616-1627 for the Hobart family of
legal note. The north side was filled in during the
1760s and 1770s and fits in with the style very well.
What you remember about so brilliant a building is
the brick with stone dressings, the turret and open
topped lantern in the centre, bay windows, turrets with
ogee tops, a very fine gallery and spacious main rooms.
Repton is thought to have done the gardens in the
later 18th century. Then of course there is the glory of
the parish church of St Andrew nearby.

a classic of the type.

LODDON

      Loddon is a very small town to the east of the
main road from Norwich to Beccles and best known to
the county and tourists for its great church of Holy
Trinity, a building of the late 15th century throughout
and with exceptional numbers and area of clerestorey
windows. The porch is especially brilliantly decorated,
and the interior of the church is awash with things of
interest: many stone monuments, stained glass, woodwork,
brasses, screen and even a painting of the late Tudor era
showing the Hobarts.

      The town has an historic core round the
church square and High Street including Georgian brick
properties, inns and the like. Loddon House is the
most notable property in the place after the church,
and this is a classical early 18th century house of some
distinction for so small a place. PLenty of new housing
developments means that the town flourishes in a quiet
way, the school is full, the shops do well and town life
in the countryside is maintained in these harsh economic
days.

      Over the little river Chet is Chedgrave, an
attractive smaller settlement close to Loddon and with
a Norman church complete with tower. And not far off
another treat for church historians, the Norman church of
Hales - St Margaret, with a round tower, nave, chancel and

WELLS NEXT THE SEA

you are the grand entrance portico, the mighty wings, the superb grounds and much else. I first saw it as a student, an impresionable industrial Lancashire undergraduate from an area with few such palaces.

        Wells is both a seaside place and a combination of port and retirement centre. It is small and really one might call it a village, but in historical terms it was a town, and it fulfills most of the criteria. Its parallel streets are linked by narrow alleys rather like those in Yarmouth (the Rows) and my holiday there was brought back to mind recently in a TV series filmed in the place and round about.

        In the town the Buttlands is a large green lined with trees and fronted by a number of fine looking Georgian houses: one end leads to the narrow alleys mentioned above. The quay area is especially agreeable in the good weather of spring and summer, when it is alive with bustle as small craft come and go: plenty of those small brick properties which so enhance a quayside without dominating or restricting. The parish church is a fine late Victorian building with tower and some old bits and pieces of the old fabric from the fire of 1879.

        Just out of town and away from the lovely beaches and coastline is Holkham Hall, the splendid brick Paladian style mansion of the Cokes, earls of Leicester, and of the period 1730-1760. What impresses

HOLT

SHERINGHAM

We used to pass through Holt on our way to the coast and Sheringham over the years. Holt has a famous school in it, Gresham's School, founded in the 1550s by that brilliant financier, founder of the stock exchange and banker, Sir Thomas Gresham - a real Elizabethan character larger than life. It used to occupy the site of Gresham's manor house - he was born and raised in Holt and generously endowed the school as thankyou to the place - but it occupies newer, far larger premises out of the centre these days. I recall the Grasshopper sign for the banker, for Martins Banks used to have them on show as their symbol.

Holt of course is more than a school: the parish church is a nice one, but in Norfolk terms decidedly second rate thanks to a fire and extensive work by William Butterfield last century. High Street and the Market Place show off the sort of pleasant town properties one would expect in a rural backwater, but out of town is Home Place, one of E S Prior's best known 1900s works, which is regarded as something of a rogue design - concrete with pebbles, thin brickwork, lavishly decorated exterior, and built at enormous expense for a clergyman.

This little town on the north Norfolk coast was my first holiday home on my travels in East Anglia and I have to admit to a partiality for the place. It comprises two distinct "towns", Lower Sheringham beside the sea, and quite new, and Upper Sheringham, the old part of the settlement. Everywhere is pleasant and nothing offends in spite of the general lack of many old buildings or ancient history.

Lower town has its seafront , promenade, extensive shingle beach, lifeboat and fishing boats, several excellent pubs, shops, and plenty of guest houses and some notable examples of c1900 hotel architecture. That was the date for most of the buildings, from the 1890s to c1914, and again in the 1920s.

Upper town is older, up on the hillside which rises surprisingly steeply from the seafront. The parish church is attractive, medieval and of several styles including a tower of the c1300 years. Out of town is Sheringham Hall, one of Humphrey Repton's successes of c1815 which he did with his son as a team effort for the Upcher family. All the plans remain - the famous Red Books outlining all that was to be done in and out to produce the present house and grounds.

Sheringham is just a nice size: our hosts on
several holidays were local folk who knew everybody and
their life centred on local work and entertainment,
but there has been a substantial influx of offcomers
into business and for retirement. Despite the fairly
modern nature of development the town has plenty of those
little back alleys and courts which are so characteristic
of fishing places, and of course there are numerous
pretty little cottages involving both brick and flint.

CROMER

Cromer has altogether more presence, more about
itself, than some other coastal places in the county,
and in recalling the town I think of the massive tower
of the parish church of St Peter and St Paul, of the
many Edwardian hotels and houses, of the boats drawn up
away from the powerful waves high on the steeply sloping
shingle beach, and of the terraces and cliffs which
do not somehow seem of the county.

The old quarter is of ancient cottages of
various 17th to 18th century dates, arranged round the
parish church which has a knapped flint tower of 160
feet, and a body of medieval and later origins and
especially impressive in its loftiness. The hotels
and larger businesses and houses show off their brickwork
of the later Victorian and early 20th century expansion
of Cromer when it was for a time very "in" as a resort:
a haunt of minor literary and society figures escaping
London and the Home Counties for a time, and today
just as popular.

Endless walks down or up the coast too, for
this is part of the lengthy Norfolk heritage coast.
The lighthouse used to be open whenever we called and
displayed its brilliant white sight to all visitors.
Inland is Felbrigg, a strange place without a proper
village, for the buildings have gone except for a

decidedly picturesque medieval church and the hall,
a big Jacobean house extended in that century and again
100 years or so later. It was in the ownership of the
Wyndhams, who carried some political clout and were
wealthy 17th and 18th century gentry.

SUFFOLK

SUFFOLK

MILDENHALL

Suffolk sits in between Norfolk and
Essex, and has something of the character of both
its neighbours, but really an identity of its own.
It is a county of gentle countryside, not much that one
could describe as spectacular: wooded districts,
lots of open land, fertile in the main, gentle
rolling areas, and above all delightful villages.
To some extent it comes into London's orbit, but
only occasionally so far as commuting is concerned,
and the county maintains a resolute economic life of
its own which has always supported a large population
since the early middle ages. It is a farming county,
but with ports and resorts on the coast, growing
amounts of tourism, and above all attracting in many
offcomers from the south east who value its pleasanter
pace of life. Suffolk does not have the great city,
like Norwich is in Norfolk; or the spreading London
towns of Essex; but it does have scores of picturesque
smaller centres, most of which you can find in the
following pages, and so often typical of the best to
be found anywhere in the country.

Mildenhall is where the great fenlands begin
in the north west corner of Suffolk going into the next
county, Cambridgeshire, so it is flat and ideal land for
the RAF and their runways. It has also attracted much
new housing and other development since the war, which
has somewhat changed the character of the district.
The Romans and their successors the Saxon tribes have
left their mark on the landscape, and Roman remains such
as those at Thistley Green have yielded substantial
amounts of information and artefacts.

People come to Mildenhall to see the church of
St Mary and St Andrew, right in the heart of the
town with a large churchyard, a tower of 120 feet and
a main body of 170 feet which makes it very large.
What you remember about the inside is the roof,
covered with animals, angels and things from the Bible,
which defied attempts by the puritans of the 17th century
to shoot them down !

The east end seems to be 13th century and the
main part of the nave 200 years later, like the tower.
There are a number of furnishings to view inside and
a charnel house outside to add interest !

It was near here that the socalled Mildenhall

treasure was found in the 1940s, a magnificent collection
of silver ware from Roman times and worth a king's ransom.

CLARE

      Clare is on the Essex border and not far from
Cambridgeshire: it is eminently picturesque with a wealth
of timber framed and timbered properties, the pargetting
or ornamental plasterwork on the outside of houses
that is such a speciality of the region, and the sort of
townscape which appeals to overseas visitors as essentially
English. Then too it has a ruined priory, long gone
castle, and lovely parish church to complete the
scene.

      Clare priory was the first house of the
Austin friars in the country, of the 1240s, and an
important establishment. It was here that royal and
noble travellers were entertained, that Edward Ist's
daughter Joan was buried in 1305, and that the Austin
friars returned in the 1950s - most unusual indeed.
Substantial parts of the house remain from the early
14th century - walls, doorways, vaulted rooms, arches,
infirmary, and so on. Very evocative place to be even
nowadays.

      The castle was early Norman, and the mound
remains though the railway occupied the inner bailey and
the priory the outer one. The parish church of St Peter
and St Paul has an extensive churchyard in the heart of
the town, and is apparently mostly a 14th and 15th century
structure with earlier tower - though considerable parts

of the earlier church remain in the newer fabric, and
there was the inevitable tinkering with the masonry in
later centuries.

Plenty of pargetting and timber properties to
delight the eye. Just look at the Grove and the Ancient
House of the 15th century, the Swan Inn, and the length
of the High Street, Market Hill and other roads. Traffic
can be dreadful, but it does not spoil the place.

LEISTON

Leiston is an industrial centre which sits
in the shadow of the vast Sizewell atomic energy plant on
the coast (though Leiston is inland of it): plenty of
work and high incomes though the penalties are obvious.
The Norman abbey for Premonstratensian canons was moved
from Minsmere Marshes to Leiston in the 1360s,
and this was a considerable house for the Order. Its
buildings of the later 14th to early 16th centuries
stillexist as substantial ruins in brick, flint
and stone, very picturesque compared to parts of the
district and its buildings.

The dissolved abbey was given by the king to
the duke of Suffolk who allowed the church to be used as
a farm. Interestingly, the Lady Chapel of the church was
restored to religious use   this century by Ellen
Wrightson, whilst parts of the old fabric are now a
meeting place for retreats and the like in the diocese -
very fitting too.

The coastal villages are dominated by the
nuclear power station, covered in aluminium, and the
plant the subject of recent years of endless debate and
investigation about a second atomic centre next door.

I have to say that I do wonder how it came to
be planted here at all, bearing in mind thé unspoilt
nature of the coast and surrounding urban and village
centres.

ALDEBURGH

        Aldeburgh, along with so many East Anglian
towns, was once a thriving port, but since the 16th
century it and most of the other little ports have
lost that function thanks to erosion by the sea. The town
is famous for its annual music festival founded in 1948
by local composer Benjamin Britten; its fame in this
respect belies the small population of a few thousand.

        The town is picturesque, with a High Street
composed of several ages of building and architectural
styles but essentially Georgian, and a Tudor Moot Hall
which was once in the town centre but is now thanks to
the gradual reclaiming of the sea, right at the sea's
edge. Many larger houses are up on the high land, and
especially on the cliffs, above the town and sea,
and bear witness to the genteel nature of the people who
started to live here in the later 18th and 19th
centuries. Then there are hotels to cater for the
degrees of society who were attracted to them too.

        I once had to work on Elizabeth Garrett
Anderson's career, she being of this town and famous for
her assault in the 1860s and 1870s on the male preserve
of medical training. Her sister Millicent was a suffragette
long before the official launch of the WSPU by the

Pankhursts.

The main parish church of St Peter and St Paul has a 14th century tower and a mainly Tudor body to it, and it was certainly the focal point for both pleasure and business in the town. It has a memorial to George Crabbe, born here in 1755, who was ordained a clergyman in 1782 after a surprising variety of jobs and occupations: he held various posts and wrote some distinguished poetry whilst living in Suffolk.

WOODBRIDGE

Woodbridge is one of the most favoured of Suffolk towns from the point of view of setting, at the head of the wide river Deben estuary, surrounded by gentle hilly and well wooded countryside, and looking extremely prosperous. The main road is bypassed now so that the web of little byways which converge on the town do not provide too much traffic for most of the year. The riverside is not that attractive thanks to industrial development in a modest way, but it is undeniably beckoning and devotees pleasure sailing love it. The place was a medieval port of note but declined in the 17th century: I once read Edward Fitzgerald's biography and how much his sailing hereabouts meant to him, "Old Fitz" as he was known.

The unusual tidal mill still exists and there is a landmark of a c1815 windmill on one of the hills. St Mary's church tower provides another viewpoint at over 100 feet, and the church is justly prized for the lavish decorative work of the 15th century. Packed with interesting artefacts, the church not surprisingly attracts visitors by the coachload.

Thomas Seckford laid the foundations for much of the good building in Woodbridge - he was the sort of rich benefactor most towns needed in the 16th

century !

        The Shire Hall is said to be one of Seckford's
but it is much altered; the King's Head inn is the sort
of jettied timber framed building that the substantial
numbers of Americans at the local airbase love to see;
and so is the Angel inn. A 1560s Elizabethan brick
mansion stands on the site of the old Augustinian priory
founded in the 1190s and bought by Seckford after the
Dissolution. The town is made up of narrow streets
which centre on the church, and the main street or
Thoroughfare which is altogether more spacious, less
intimate and medieval, and with the feel of a later
Georgian and early Victorian route. Everywhere you
look there are old properties, and usually in a fine
state of repair. Altogether a very fortunate town for
the way its heritage has been preserved.

SOUTHWOLD

        One of the delights of any Suffolk holiday is
going to visit Southwold on the coast, one of the very
nicest of resorts and a brilliant and succesful blend
of ancient and modern, extensive grass and greens with
water and sea, and above all a townscape of modest
properties with little out of place in what has
grown up to be a happy environment for both tourist and
resident.

        The town's harbour is small but lively,
the beach pebble and sand, and the medieval wealth of the
town based on its fishing and port functions as well as
its servicing the farming and woollen districts.
Wealth was abundant and hence the glories 15th
century parish church of St Edmund in superb flushwork -
the decorative use of flint along with stone to make
patterns, and something of a Suffolk speciality.
It is majestic and a real tourist trap at times -
everyone seems to have heard of its beauty.

        The town has no outstanding building apart from
the church, but this does not matter since it is to be
savoured as a whole, an entity, helped by its spaciousness
thanks to the combination of fires and planning over
the centuries. Brick and flint with colour washed
properties make it all so jolly, so pretty: High Street,

Church Street,   the Market Place, the Greens, are typical
of the routes to be walked - though it takes some time
thanks to the spacious quality.   No end of Georgian
and Victorian properties mingle with late medieval
and 17th century ones -   the Swan Hotel, Greyfriars,
a small Methodist chapel, the manor house, and Hill House
are typical of what the town has to offer in the way of
architectural pleasures.   Even a brilliantly white
Victorian lighthouse is acceptable. I should
mention the extensive riverside area, almost a lake,
which cuts deep into the countryside, and the extensive
cliffs on part of the coast too which add so much
character to any resort.

HALESWORTH

        Inland of Southwold and along the little river
Blyth is Halesworth, one of those middling Suffolk
market towns, but in this case unusual in that it
enjoyed considerable expansion thanks to the development
of the Blyth navigation for shipping in the 18th
century and the coming of the railways in the 19th.
Sadly it means that much of the ancient part of the
town has gone and lots of modern development of the
last 150 years exists.

        The parish church is of several medieval
dates but the appearance is Victorian thanks to
repeated additions and alterations last century.
Nice 15th century tower however, and the interior offers
brasses, sculptures, woodwork and all that a good
parish church should offer to its tourist visitors.

        The town does have old buildings but not in
enormous numbers or even in rows, so that it is a bit
disappointing that old sits not with old. However
you can enjoy the 17th century almshouses, several
timber framed medieval properties including the old
rectory, the Maltings round an old courtyard and looking
charming, and occasional old shop fronts not always
in imitation details but sometimes original 18th and
early 19th century.

Down the road is Huntingfield, once the home of
the Paston family who were so important in regional
affairs in the middle ages and later.

BUNGAY

Amongst the more noticeable names of the county
is Bungay, set on the river Waveney and much involved in
today's leisure craft and yachting industry for tourists.
For several centuries the town was a market centre for
the district and in the 18th century commenced the
famous local industry of printing, surprisingly enough.
The castle was built by the Bigods c1150 during the
ferocious 19 years of war of Stephen's reign: a fine
curtain wall, the usual defences, big keep and with that
rarest of survivals, a mining gallery designed to
bring down the (isolated) tower on to the enemy at the
moment of their success. All very impressive indeed.

The open octagonal market cross or butter
cross is in the Market Place, and is a handsome classical
item put up after the usual great town fire c1688.
The streets show off an excellent choice of old properties
but the feel is Georgian, and of the 18th century, in
what was a prosperous town spending money after fire
damage. Thus St Mary's Street district, Bridge Street,
Earsham Street, and others have rows of good town houses
and cottages which belie their years so far as their
condition goes.

The town had a Benedictine priory for nuns
founded in the 1180s and enjoying modest wealth and

importance. Its extensive buildings continued in use
until the late 17th century fire mentioned which took
down the lot apart from the nave of the church. This
continues to be used as the town's parish church,
which is a notable building complete with grand
tower, flushwork, and masonry of several medieval
centuries. That is St Mary's, but the town benefits too
from Holy Trinity, which has a Norman round tower
and medieval nave, though a 20th century chancel.
Each is most pleasant to sit in provided it is not too
packed with tourists.

SAXMUNDHAM

        To some extent like an overgrown village,
the little town of Saxmundham straddles the main road
between Ipswich and Lowestoft, a few miles inland from
the coast. It was a coaching centre in a modest sort
of way , and in the main street the principal buildings
seem to be the little former town hall and the big
inn, the Bell Hotel. What you remember about the parish
church is the work of the great sculptors Nollekens and
Westmacott of the early 19th century, providing fitting
memorials for the local dignitaries. The church
itself is indeterminate medieval and of several
dates and styles.

        Out of town are the Glenhams. Little
Glenham has one of those interesting parish churches
with Norman origins and rebuilt gradually over the
ceturies, plus an early 18th century hall of
brick - quite lovely with its gardens in the summer
sun. Great Glenham has its big house, this time a
house not a hall, and in grey brick which does not
seem to suit it so well: but a charming composition of
1814, and All Saints church once more is a happy
agglomeration of styles.

FELIXSTOWE

Felixstowe suddenly developed as a seaside
resort in the 1890s and 1900s, thus the many substantial
houses , hotels, business premises and resort development
of the Edwardian era, and often in red brick. It
retains its resort functions today, but so much is
given over to the port work, to local industrial and
factory concerns, and to such work as offices and
schools. Ipswich of course is just up the road,
and the delights of the several river estuaries round the
corner on both sides. ·

Felixstowe since the last war has become one
of the busiest of container ports placed on this
eastern part of the country and with its twin , Harwich,
just across the rivers Stour and Orwell. It is
an ancient settlement, having once had a Roman fort,
now under the sea, and a Benedictine monastery, founded
about 1105 by Roger Bigod, earl of Norfolk, and
one of the outposts of the great house at Rochester
cathedral. It was one of those houses suppressed by
the domineering Cardinal Wolsey in 1528 in order to
divert the revenues to his new college at Ipswich - but he
fell from grace soon after and the property went to the
favoured (but eventually also doomed !) duke of
Norfolk.

Landguard fort guards the harbour, one of
those 16th century efforts against possible French invasion
and rebuilt several times in the 17th, 18th and 19th
centuries as threat succeeded threat: quite a lot
of old work to see there too. A Martello tower for
lookouts and defences and of c1810 also stands on the
front. What is called Old Felixstowe is small, with the
parish church at the heart and various attractive cottages
and houses round about and from several centuries.

LOWESTOFT

In the swinging 60s as an impressionable
sixthformer I took coach from industrial Lancashire to
spend a holiday at a holiday camp in Lowestoft for
two weeks, and having to walk everywhere, I came to
know the place rather better than would normally have been
the case. The old town has spread enormously, and
especially to the south and Pakefield, this century,
for it is a popular fishing port and holiday and
retirement resort, and keeps pace with Yarmouth just to
the north and over the county boundary. It is the most
easterly part of England, and I recall the vast stretches
of beach, the seemingly endless sand dunes, sea and sky
that make holidays provided the weather is good (as it
was !).

Plenty of parks, pleasure places, hotels, guest
houses, new housing and industrial estates and sites,
intense activity round Oulton Broad as it emerges from
the land to the sea , piles of traffic, a forest of
boats moored, all add up to a thoroughly enjoyable urban
experience. No lack of churches for various denominations
but all dwarfed by St Margaret's 120 foot spire and a
body of not far short of 200 feet - a very fine building
of the later middle ages which speaks volumes for the
wealth of the port in those times.

Whilst there on my last trip I saw how much the
local Lowestoft porcelain had appreciated in value !
The firm was established in the town in 1757 in what is
now Crown Street, and went out of business in 1802 after
producing some excellent blue and white ware as well
as such things as inkstands, small bowls and tea caddies
especially for Georgian tourists.   Lowestoft folk
are proud of their porcelain factory which for a while
put the town on the porcelain map.

Benjamin Britten the composer was born and
raised in Lowestoft: and Polish born Joseph Conrad,
writer of so many well known novels, landed here in
1878 as a young man - he put the town and district
in at least one of his books.

BECCLES

to the staithe or quayside on the river with its leisure
craft to enjoy. From what I recall there is a regatta
held here in the summer which attracts crowds, but usually
Beccles is a user-friendly place without too many tourists
to ruin it for the residents, and everywhere a feeling
of that wellbeing which pervades so many of the county's
middling market towns.

        Beccles lies just to the south of the
broad river Waveney as it heads for the sea right by
the Norfolk border. The river used to be navigable but
during the middle ages one of those customary silting ups
took place and left the town high and dry. The big parish
church of St Michael is the star attraction partly because
of its bold outline against the sky from most viewpoints,
and although it contains early medieval work, the fabric
is mainly a late 15th and early 16th century rebuilding.
What you recall about the church is the ambitious
porch on the south side, a detached church tower of
about 100 feet well away from the body of the building,
and an exterior more interesting than the interior.
The latter was seriously damaged in fire in the 16th
century, as was the town on several occasions so that
not much dates from before the 17th century.

        A nice villagey town hall of the 1720s, of
brick, graces the town centre and round it various brick
and timber framed cottages and houses which look
17th and 18th century. St Peter's House is one of the
most imposing properties, Georgian brick and typically
attractive.

        A very pleasant walk may be had along Northgate,
Saltgate, the Old Market, Ballygate, Newmarket, and down

LAVENHAM

Is Lavenham the most beautiful of all East
Anglian towns, with the most beautiful of all churches ?
Many would argue thus, and how about living in this
wonderful creation of the wool and cloth wealth of
the middle ages ? Tourists flock here in numbers to
drink of the loveliness.

The church of St Peter and St Paul looks to
be a product of the late medieval years, that is late 15th
and early 16th century, and mostly paid for by the town's
clothiers (especially the Spring family) and the earl of
Oxford, John de Vere. The tower is 140 feet and the
length of the church 156, so that the former does seem to
dwarf the latter - and the place thus loses points
to its close rival Long Melford - but the whole ensemble
has a unity of design and nobility of scale and purpose
that otherwise it is hard to fault. An interior that is
all light and spaciousness and the match of any in the
Cotswolds, and packed with top quality woodwork and other
furnishings :   brasses and stone monuments stand out in
the memory.

The town is a delight: amongst the best buildings
is the Guildhall of c1530, a big and ornate timber
structure for the Guild of Corpus Christi. Water Street,
Shilling Street, Barn Street, the Market Place,
Church Street and others   display the sort of houses

built by the wool merchants from their wealth of the
14th and 15th centuries, and that have remarkably survived
500 years somehow. Presumably the wealth of medieval
Lavenham was never again available and the town became
a Suffolk backwater over the last 300 years, thus
avoiding any harmful development, industry and housing
concerns that would have ruined its homogeneity.

What about the beauty of the Wool Hall, or the
Swan Hotel, or Woolstaplers , or the old grammar school ?
Plus a number of Georgian brick houses and premises which
complement the whole pattern of architecture rather than
rival or ruin it. Well done Lavenham !

its near neighbour down the road, Clare. They make
interesting constrasts !

HAVERHILL

        Haverhill is right on the Essex border and not
that far from the London web of towns, and it was chosen
to be one of those new development towns of the postwar
era to relieve population pressures in the capital
city. The result has been that the small town has
grown enormously in the last 40 years with extensive
new housing and industrial estates all over the place.
Your impression after visiting it may well be that
old Haverhill has gone and that what is old is more or
less Victorian, with vast amounts of modern work.

        The parish church is reasonably impressive
and medieval but substantially altered after a fire in
the 1660s and inevitably in last century so that there
is not that interest either inside or out which
characterises most Suffolk parish churches. The monument
to John Ward stands out, and it is 16th century.

        Odd bits and pieces of the historic past of
the town remain - Weavers Row of 12 medieval cottages is
an example - and here of course cloth and wool were
the staple employment as in most of Suffolk. In the
surrounding countryside are many Suffolk villages with
more interesting historic buildings, and especially
churches, and one cannot help but compare Haverhill to

NEEDHAM MARKET

St John Baptist church was built at the expense
of the bishop of Ely in the 1460s or 1470s, and its
vastly complex, intricate, beautiful and brilliant
roof is described as the finest achievement of carpenters
in the country. It is a hammerbeam one with the beams
sticking out all over the place and dominating the
entire building - it appears that the reasonably plain
stone church went up just to show off the roof: when
you bear in mind this was a chapel of ease until this
century, the cost and extravagance of this roof is
amazing. You need to see it to understand its detailed
complexity.

Needham is close by the main routes to and from
Ipswich and Stowmarket, with the latter a near neighbour
and much larger. The town presents a High Street and
minor roads full of old properties including many timber
framed later medieval examples and some typical of the
Georgian era in their classical details and brickwork.
It is not of course like Lavenham for instance where there
is an embarrassment of riches , but it does have its
good buildings and the town was, as might be expected,
a wool and cloth centre in the middle ages. It was also
a coaching centre too, the last change of horses before
the gallop into Ipswich or the first stop and pick up on
the way out to Bury or the north. Just look at some of
the inns too - the Bull is usually cited as an excellent
example of the old coaching inn.

Strangely enough the 1630s grammar school
which is also timber framed, was built from the demolished
remains of the old guildhall of the town. There are
early 19th century almshouses which attempt to fake
the 16th century, and one of those picturesque Quaker
meeting houses complete with old yard and headstones in
the simple form beloved of the Society of Friends. It
is the parish church however which draws the tourists.

EYE

Eye is a few miles south of the Norfolk border
and on the little river Dove. Yet another market town
which grew to wealth on the backs of sheep, Eye has
much to offer the tourist in the way of places to view.
People perhaps come most to see the parish church of
St Peter and St Paul, with its splendid tower of 100
feet and all in local flushwork (flint and stone
patterns) and of the 15th century. As was so often
the case the town rebuilt an earlier structure - in this
town probably 13th century, when money was also plentiful
(it was the black death of the 1340s ruined things in
so many ways, including church building for a time)
and so there is a juxtapositioning of styles to create
quite a masterpiece - though not one of the grandest
of Suffolk churches.

The medieval rood screen has here been restored
to what it may well have looked like in the middle
ages - they were nearly all destroyed in the 16th century
as so many forms of idolatry and papist works - and I
think that it was Sir Ninian Comper who did the work
earlier this century.

The little town has its memorable buildings apart
from the parish church. A notable guildhall of the

early Tudor years and (of course) timber framed,
and with lots of carving. Tudor House nearby is
actually Georgian brick, but presumably this is a new
facade (as was so often the case) on a late medieval
structure. There was a Norman castle in the town but
only the mound and earthworks remain. Of the Georgian
properties, Linden House is the most superior: the town
seems to have enjoyed prosperity in the 18th century
even after cloth and wool had gone into decline locally
(though moving to.Yorkshire in fact).

If you leave behind the pleasant Georgian and
timber framed late medieval streets of Eye, walk out to
the ruined Benedictine priory founded about 1080 by
Robert Malet, for monks, and an alien priory which
paid a hefty fine to become native (or denizen).
A farm is on the site today with some ruins: the monks
had much income from Dunwich but sea damage took away
most of their income in the 15th century and the place
never recovered.

FRAMLINGHAM

Framlingham seems to be, according to the map,
at the centre of all the local roads and routes. It
was the ancient seat of the Bigods, earls of Norfolk
in Norman times, but Henry IInd pulled down their
castle in the 1170s thanks to the family's constant
planning of revolts against the king. In easier times
the Bigods were allowed to rebuild c1200, and thanks
to experiences in the Crusades, Roger Bigod built one
of the first defensive curtain walls in the country
though not that long after its completion the royal
line took it off them again: thereafter it had various
constables until becoming Howard property, part of that
family's vast possessions.

The castle hit hard times in the 16th century
when the Howards were out of favour and went through
various ownerships, ending up with Pembroke college
and all save for the gatehouse, walls and towers more or
less totally demolished. A sad fate indeed. Still,
like Kenilworth, it is a most impressive ruin.

The town has a splendid 15th and 16th century
parish church, St Michael's, though with older masonry
especially in the chancel end. The magnificence of such
things as the roof, furnishings and flushwork is due to
the Howards being buried here in some numbers. The

monuments to the Howards are also, as would be expected,
famous: they include dukes and earls and their ladies,
plus the illegitimate son of Henry VIII, the duke of
Richmond. They form a rich and fascinating display of
Howard wealth and the skill of masons especially in the
early 16th century.

Though the little town has its late medieval
houses and a number of the 16th and 17th century, what
you recall about the town is its wealth of Georgian into
Regency houses - some very distinctive quality properties
in Castle Street, Church Street, Market Hill and so on,
and that sign of a local wealthy middle class society,
a Unitarian chapel.

STOWMARKET

show off some good old coaching inns and premises as
well as houses: predominantly 18th and early 19th
century, spurred on to rebuilding medieval structures by
coaching business and then by railway impetus c1840.
No lack of Victorian buildings too in what was an
economy not just reliant on agriculture. One of the
nicest of county museums is in the town these days
to be enjoyed by tourists.

        Not that far out of Ipswich and on the way
to Bury St Edmunds is Stowmarket, a town which now combines
residential functions for increasing numbers of people
with its market and industrial expansion of recent
decades. It is also a tourist place, and has in the
parish church of St Mary and St Peter a very attractive
church: mainly of the 15th century including the tower,
but with earlier work on view and a happy combination
of interest both in and out. It has a collection of
monuments of quality, many to the Tyrrells, and will
occupy an hour or two of your time.

        Funnily enough the local hospital,
Stow Lodge, was built as the new workhouse c1780 under
an attempt to curb poverty in rural districts thanks to
the Gilbert Act (replaced by the New poor Law of the
1830s): it was a measure to force all in receipt of
poor rate into the building where they endured a very
harsh life and had to work hard too - out-relief for
the poor in their own homes was discouraged.   A wide
red brick in severest Georgian classical.

        The Market Place and the main roads in and out

SUDBURY

Sudbury is stuck in my memory as the original
of EATANSWILL in Dickens' PICKWICK PAPERS of the 1830s,
a portrait of a totally corrupt and rotten borough at a
parliamentary election ! It is also the birthplace of
the illustrious Thomas Gainsborough in 1727, one
of the greatest of painters   not finding fame here but
in London society. The town was a Saxon burgh mentioned
in that seminal work THE ANGLO SAXON CHRONICLE and
was integrated into the life and work of the surrounding
countryside: in the middle ages it was a cloth town,
and today it offers a safe haven for many offcomers who
want to live within striking distance of Ipswich and
Colchester, or far enough from the London orbit which
begins not far over the county boundary in Essex.

The parent church of the town is St Gregory
(which name suggests a Saxon foundation in the 7th century
dedicated to Pope Gregory the Great the man who sent
Augustine to mission England), and this is the third
fabric on the same site, more or less rebuilt by
local man Archbishop Simon of Sudbury c1370. He also
founded a college of priests to work what was a very
populated area: from what I recall it was he who was
murdered whilst interceding in the Peasants Revolt of
1381, and his preserved head is in this church !

Sudbury has several medieval churches.
St Gregory's is later 14th century but altered in the
1480s, and is of flint - very becoming indeed with its
tower. St Peter's was a chapel to it, which for a
chapel of ease to Gregory's suggests general munificence
locally - a large and ornate church which cost a lot to
build. Both these churches were assailed by William
Butterfield last century as he carried out work.

Another 15th century chapel is All Saints,
a third fine building - quite remarkable in so small
a town, and bearing witness to cloth and wool
profits. The town displays its corn exchange, several
banks and the like as signs of continuing prosperity
tied in with farming. Plenty of Georgian brickwork is
to be enjoyed, including Gainsborough's birthplace.
Sufficient of those later medieval timber framed properties
including jettied ones, to show that the merchants also
spent lavishly on their own comforts too. The Moot
Hall is a good example of this.

The town had those symbols of medieval
urban success, the friars, here in the early 13th
century - Dominicans, and an important house devoted
to theologians and education. It had many well known
friars within its walls including heads of the Order.
Not much remains of it though.

There was a small Benedictine cell for monks
dating from the 1100s and founded by Henry's
master of the mint, Wulfric. Again little remains to
be viewed.

A most enjoyable town in which to wander
for the tourist.

IPSWICH

The principal commercial and industrial town
of Suffolk lies on the south east tip of the county
at the head of the river Orwell's estuary. It gets its
name from the river being known as the Gipping higher
up and has long been a settlement of importance from
before the Roman invasions. It was the main port of the
district and county throughout the middle ages and
enjoyed considerable wealth which showed in its having
many medieval churches and large timber framed merchants'
properties. During the 16th and 17th centuries decline
set in (as it did in much of the region) thanks to the
loss of the wool and cloth trade: quiet times too
in the 18th century, but during the 19th century the
port, thanks to railways, blossomed forth once more
and over the last 150 years the functions of industrial
and commercial centre have boomed. Population may well
have been towards 10,000 c1500, but was only 11,000
in 1801: this century it has more than doubled from
60,000 to 120,000 and more.

I always associate the town with Cardinal
Wolsey, son of a local butcher and holder of more
wealth and power than the king in the 1520s before his
sudden fall. He gave his king an early example of how
to get rid of monasteries by suppressing 7 to found his
Ipswich college, but the project was never completed.

The town also had Franciscan, Dominican and
Carmelite friaries from the early 13th century through
to 1538, all of them of considerable importance to their
national Orders, with good libraries, outstanding
friars in their numbers, and substantial wealth.
Some of the whole buildings remained into last century
but little beyond odd arches and parts of walls is
left today.

Ipswich had two Augustinian priories, each of
them sizeable. Once more sadly little or nothing
remains beyond piles of stones and bits of walling.

The churches fared rather better and the town
is rich in medieval fabrics. St Lawrence is 15th century
at the height of the town's wealth. It has a very ornate
flushwork tower of 100 feet. St Margaret's is the best
regarded of the churches, a fine structure of the 14th
century and embellished in true decorated, lavish,
style. Other medieval chruches include St Mary Stoke,
which suffered various substantial later alterations,
St Mary at the Quay, of the 15th century, and St Nicholas.
There are others, and a mountain of Victorian churches
and chapels.

The Dissenters were and are strongly represented
as in most commercial centres: lovely c1700 Unitarian,
that is Dissenting, chapel, is about the nicest.

Unfortunately the main civic buildings appear
to be wholly Victorian - Corn Exchange, town hall,
custom house and so on, though the shire hall was once
the county gaol ! Christchurch Mansion is now the
star of the secular buildings, a real mansion of c1550
remodelled and extended in the c1670 years - now a
splendid museum and art gallery in a lovely setting of
garden and trees, and on the site of one of the Austin
priories.

The Ancient House in the Butter Market is
one of the memorable houses of the county: awash with
pargetting (carved plasterwork) and arguably the best
extant example of that art form. The house is c1567
and reminds the tourist of the wealth of that time.

Ipswich has expanded remarkably.in the last
century and modern development is everywhere. The old
historic core remains but has been breached by many
roads and new buildings: you can still enjoy a walk
in Cornhill (the market place), the Butter Market,
Brook Street, and especially Fore Street with its
collection of excellent 16th and 17th century houses.
Any number of old inns too, lovely looking and inviting
shop fronts , a wealth of town houses on what were once
crowded town sites.

BURY ST EDMUNDS

Bury is the county town of West Suffolk, the
great county rival to Ipswich, and so much more of
the county and county life to many than is that far
larger Ipswich with its industry and commerce and modern
expansion.   Bury is to many the great abbey of St
Mary and St Edmund, one of the greatest 4 or 5
Benedictine houses of Britain, and with today just the
groundplan and two gates surviving along with parts of
walls and the like. When you bear in mind that the
site measures over 1500 feet by 1000 you can see how
grand it all was.

The first monastery dates from the earlier 7th
century the heroic age of Saxon missionary work amongst
the East Angles : in the 920s it was reformed as a college
for secular priests, and c1020 King Canute made it
Benedictine again with 20 monks. The house rose higher
in royal favour and was made one of 80 monks by William
the Conqueror, which meant a community of hundreds of
people. It was used for parliament   on a number of
occasions in the later 13th and other centuries, was
quite exceptionally rich, and produced many eminent
monks including the 12th century writer   Jocelin.
All that remains are extensive ruins plus the two great
gates, plenty of walling and the like, and lots of written
material.

The little town grew in the shadow of the monastery but there was a catalogue of trouble between the two including serious, murderous riots twice, with the abbey burned down. Partly jealousy , partly the power and wealth, caused problems and poor peasants were easily encouraged: the wealth of the place can be gauged from the size of the church, which at 500 feet long with a west front of 250 feet was far larger than most cathedrals including Norwich !

Bury of course is St Edmundsbury, where the king and martyr Edmund was buried after being killed by the Danes in 869: his shrine attracted many to the abbey and brought money too. Edmund was also for many years patron saint of England. The town grew out of the abbey, and in Norman times the place was laid out on an ambitious, and still obvious, plan by the monks - over 350 houses were up c1090. It is a marvellous place for walking round despite the traffic: just look at the delightful Angel Hill which has the Athenaeum and ballroom of the 1700s and later. All around is a spacious open area lined with Georgian properties of real quality.

The Suffolk hotel is c1800 and serves to show the prosperity from coaching and of the town at that time. The Traverse displays fine 17th century timber framed houses; admire the mix of styles and building materials too in Guildhall Street, St Mary's Square, Churchgate Street, and Baxter Street - it is not possible to name all the houses because there really are hundreds to see.

Of major buildings there is the town hall which was one of Robert Adam's lesser known triumphs, and at first in the 1770s a theatre. Moyse's Hall is a museum, a Norman house with later work but one of the most important domestic buildings of the region. The shire hall and similar Victorian and modern buildings are rather less notable !

Churches too abound: St James became the cathedral of the new diocese in 1914, a big church mainly of c1500   and much added to in recent decades as the work of the diocese demanded. Many tourists prefer St Mary's which is the larger church with 14th century tower and mainly 15th century fabric to the nave and chancel. It actually seems to be a prettier and more impressive sight too, and seems to have far more inside to see than the cathedral. A number of good Dissenting places of worship also grace the town including a very fine Quaker and an excellent Presbyterian (Dissenting) pair of the 18th century.

So important a town has its literary connections: Edward Fitzgerald was at school here in the 1820s. Charles Dickens was here several times staying in local inns whilst he gave readings and gathered material. Inevitably Celia Fiennes and Daniel Defoe penned their thoughts c1700 about the place after their visits on extensive tours; and down the road at Ickworth is one of the most splendid of mansions, a c1800 bizarre palace for Bishop Frederick Harvey, earl of Bristol and bishop of Derry in Ireland. Bearing in mind the house is 700 feet long and 100 high, totally influenced by the bishop's extensive Italian tours (and imprisonment !), one should expect the unexpected !

If you look at your map Bury is awash with main and minor roads arriving and departing: it is a place of much administrative work, some industry, above all a farming and county servicing station, and packed with tourists.

ESSEX

ESSEX

Essex displays the welcome diversity to be
found even in a county which has lost so much of its
territory to the encroachments of London over the
centuries. The north of the county just falls into
travelling range for commuting, and people do indeed
make the thankless daily journey there and back to
the Great Wen: but far more people live locally, and
the rich countryside is interspersed with the sort of
medieval wool and cloth towns usually associated with
Norfolk and Suffolk. Essex has its good looking
countryside, and it also has a substantial stretch of
coastline rangning from extensive mud flats, estuaries,
and spacious sand or shingle beaches, to major
ports and holiday resorts of the kind to be associated
with Blackpool ! The towns offer variety too:
industrial ones, tourist ones, utterly picturesque
ones, but all worthwhile to visit except on Bank
Holidays ! London's population of course has badly
affected the districts nearer the great city,
and there the towns are simply places to house
folk easily.

SAFFRON WALDEN

One of the most ancient towns of East Anglia as well as one of the loveliest is Saffron Walden, set in the north of the county and not far south of Cambridge. It is a blend of cloth and wool wealth from the middle ages which shows in the famously beautiful church , the old inns, and the timber framed and pargetted houses and cottages, and of later, usually Georgian, buildings that add so much to any market town. Walden priory was a house of Benedictine monks established in about 1140 by Geoffrey de Mandeville, earl of Essex, and raised to abbey status c1190. It was endowed with the income and tithes of 19 churches and much else, and was a very substantial complex of buildings. Sadly not a single thing of it exists, today because Audley End was built c1600 in best brick for the earl of Suffolk, Thomas Howard.

Audley is a star attraction, a mansion of great splendour especially inside, though a large part of the later building was altered and some demolished. To some extent the Howards were the local squires, a very grand family who led the nobility of the nation, and who here took the place of the abbey as landowners. It was wool and cloth which brought wealth, but there was the extensive growing of Saffron for yellow   dye, fields of a crocus type of plant of much commercial value.

Parts of the castle from Norman times exist and there is a museum attached. Castle Street runs from it and is awash with medieval cottages and houses that make the place most picturesque. Of larger properties Myddleton Place and Eight Bells must stand as examples of timber framing and craftsmanship on the highest scale possible. Church Street, High Street and Bridge Street display medieval and later architecture with particualr emphasis on Georgian facades, often simply placed on the front of what the Georgians thought of as unbearably old fashioned medieval timber.

The parish church is one of those brilliant examples of later medieval work with few rivals in the county. Noble tower with spire, 200 feet of body, substantial south porch, magnificent clerestorey, lovely arcading, roof of famous quality, and a richness of carvings and decoration throughout make a truly memorable sight.

Of individual buildings a few need mentioning. The Sun Inn displays what is regarded as the best pargetting in the country. The Market Place shows off many new shop fronts installed in Georgian and earlier buildings and remains the focal point for town life. The Cross keys and the Rose and Crown are two of a whole handful of notable hostelries. The town's youth hostel must be amongst the oldest in Britain, and amongst the most picturesque.

If you want to enjoy an historic town in Essex, then this is it: it has the lot !

A final note on Audley End and its glories.

At Audley the Howards held splendid court for the royalty and nobility over the centuries. Elizabethan worthies all came to stay, and in the next century men of the calibre and quality of Samuel Pepys visited and wrote down their comments in diaries and letters. Sir John Vanbrugh was the brilliant man of many parts who carried out much new work inside and outside in the early 18th century: he was man of

letters, playwrite, soldier and man of the world,
and creator of so many famous buildings .

Out of town, and there are scores of
attractive and historic villages with their manor
houses, parish churches and rows of cottages to be
enjoyed, including that gem Finchingfield, regarded
as the best of all.

EPPING

ON our first trip to see Epping Forest we were
disappointed, for like Sherwood in Nottingham, most of
the trees have gone along with much of the open space
which formed a "forest" (which did not necessarily have
endless trees).   Main roads cut through it, towns
and villages have spread across it, and being on the
edge of London does not help its present or future.
6,000 acres of open land officially exist, having been
saved from destruction in the 1880s and made over to
a public trust to preserve ; even so, 90% of it
had gone by the date compared with the 17th century.

The actual town of Epping served the scattered
forest community for centuries in what was remotest
countryside. Though there are indeed a number of
 architecturally interesting, even distinguished,
local buildings, modern and Victorian growth has been
destructive of what one would call the centre.
Several nice churches include Epping Upland church
which is celebrated for its tunnel ceiling of over
100 feet long by 20 wide, and   strong tower.

HARLOW

       I remember a film about Harlow New Town some
20 years ago or more which presented the whole plan
and place as one of enormous excitement, opportunity
and how the future would be unveiled through its
development. One wonders how the locals feel about
it all now ?   It is certainly a hive of activity,
packed with people, housing and industry, and
presumably at or nearing full maturity as an architectural
and town planning concept. What used to worry me about
new towns was the way the creators rarely ever lived
in them !

       Harlow was developed as one of the 8 new towns
planned to relieve London pressure since the 1940s,
and this time to the north of Epping, alongside the
M11 and beyond the new M25. It is on an ancient site,
this having been a Roman town and settlement: in the
middle ages it grew as a small market town, and the
present old Harlow has a true centre complete with
High Street lined with a good many Georgian properties
and earlier.

       Old Harlow has its old inns and pubs dating
from the medieval centuries into the early 19th; it has
an interesting 18th century Dissenting, Baptist, chapel;
several parish churches which incorporate or are mainly
of pre-1800 and having ancient stone and timber
framing as well as interesting furnishings;
and the curious remains of the crossing of the Norman
priory church of Latton.

       Latton was a house of Augustinian canons
founded in the 12th century, but it was not a large,
rich or successful house and in serious 15th century
decay: it hung on till the 1530s and disappeared without
a murmur. The remains of the church became a barn, of
all things.

WALTHAM ABBEY

The abbey church has oceans of things to
see: not just the Norman architecture, but the stained
glass, monuments and sculptures, paintings, and
woodwork. The town itself displays good buildings too
though expansion this century has been considerable.
Georgian houses and cottages mix with older buildings
of several dates, and there are the usual pubs, inns,
shops and premises one would expect in an historic
town. Brick mingles with weather boarding, timber
framed with stone.

Separated from main London conurbations by a
narrow stretch of countryside is Waltham Abbey,
once containing within its boundaries much of
Epping Forest. Its main claim to history is that
a church was founded by the standard bearer of King Canute,
Tofig or Toni, early in the 11th century in thanks for
finding a precious holy cross which was stored in the
church. Harold, later king, made ita college of
secular canons in the 1060s, and in fact his body,
after Hatsings, was buried here. Henry IInd made the
body into a house of Augustinian canons (and thus
monastic), and within a few years it was an abbey and
had enormous wealth which made it in the top
6 of the nation's houses.

Waltham town grew up round this great house,
which attracted many royal and noble visitors and
 patrons and had a splendid set of relics, of riches,
and of buildings. When you recall that the church
was 400 feet long you can see the splendour that has
been lost. Today 7 bays of the nave, about 100 feet,
of the Norman church of the 1100s and later, survives
as the parish church, plus very fine 14th century Lady
Chapel, crypt, with the gatehouse and bits of other
parts. It was one of the major houses of the region
and county and a trip to see it is essential.

COLCHESTER

One of the most historic cities of the nation, Colchester is, surprisingly, not a county town. It is ancient and there was a prehistoric settlement here long before the Celts arrived and made it their centre too. Next came the Romans who built their city here, the one which Boudicca burned down and where she carried out her enormous slaughter - though it was not long before the Roman empire caught up with her and both she and her army were destroyed. The defences were rebuilt by the Romans and it was one of the principal cities of the country for 3 centuries. How much it remained a city after c410 when the Romans had gone is hard to say, and there presumably continued urban life of sorts through Anglo-Saxon and Danish eras.

Colchester did well under the late Saxons judging by its importance in 1066 when the Normans triumphed at Hastings. It was in Domesday with several thousand residents, and the Normans built their enormously strong castle here which dwarfs all other keeps . At 100 feet high and measuring 150 by 110 feet, with 12 foot tapering stone walls, its size is monumental and impresses the tourists. It is built on Roman stone foundations too: what a good advert !

Hand in hand with castle building went monastic institutions for the Normans .

St John's abbey for Benedictine monks was established in Colchester in 1096 and was permanently colonised from York after Rochester monks disliked the place ! It was an important house but one much troubled throughout its 450 years of life: constant bickering and trouble with the city authorities and townsfolk, arrest of abbots and monks, problems with fire and floods, and the last abbot hanged for resisting the Dissolution. All that remains is the magnificent 15th century gatehouse in a superb show of flint workmanship: if the rest had been like this ...

The priory of St Botolph was founded for Augustinian canons about 1100, and something of a star for this was the first house of this numerous order in the entire country. It was a very important house, because of this, and given jurisdiction over the Order throughout England: even so it too was in constant disputes in the town and especially with the Benedictine abbey. All that now exists are some quite magnificent parts of the original nave of flint and Roman brick, showing the sort of c1100 architecture to great effect: again if only some more had survived, what a showpiece !

The two friaries , of Crutched and of Franciscan orders, have left not a thing to show for their 300 years of existence.

The city was a vibrant place thanks to all this religious life, and to its economic strength. Cloth gave enormous wealth in the middle ages, and just as the industry was decaying in the 16th century, hundreds of Huguenot cloth and other workers settled here and in the district to infuse new life . In that era and later centuries Colchester was a major garrison town handy for the sea, ports, London and abroad, and thousands of troops might be on hand at any one time. The consequent work and money brought here was considerable. A few local specialities might be mentioned too so far as work goes: many engineering firms in the last 200 years have found a home here, whilst plant and garden nursery businesses have thrived in Colchester and district. Oysters have provided

much interest , income and food over the centuries with
elaborate ceremonies at one time.

The town is awash with buildings and places of
interest including museums, castle, abbey-priory
ruins and the like. I should add that the new
university of Essex is just out of town, a suitable
reminder that the radical present and future live
here with the past ! Quite a tourist attraction
for people too, and much to see in the way of facilities
and architecture.

The town has extensive network of rivers and
streams, and these have been much used for industries
such as that of the various cloth processes. Amongst
the most interesting are Bourne Mill of the 1590s, once
a house and later a mill, and Cannock mill, each in
working order from memory and, of course, water
powered.

East and West Stockwell Streets are, like
a few others, packed with fascinating nooks and
crannies that can only be properly explored on
foot, and with a wealth of Georgian and earlier
properties fronting on to the pavement and usually in
brick. The same is partly true of the High Street
and East Hill but here there is more of a compromise
with the need for modern facilities - thus Victorian
and 20th century have intruded, but not ruined, the
old quarter.

Of churches, All Saints has a medieval tower and
was a museum when I was there. St Helen's chapel is
also medieval and a store. Holy Trinity is possibly the
jewel, for here is Saxon work on the tower and elsewhere
and using Roman bricks. No lack of 19th century places
of worship and many for the Dissenting community - this
was a puritan region in the 17th and 18th centuries,
and this rubbed off on to even the Anglicans of the
time.

There are a number of good old inns and
pubs with the Red Lion being typical of the timbered
late medieval structures, and very user-friendly !

The town has grown so much that it has swallowed a
number of former quite distinct parishes, many of them
with their own identity in spite of this and forming
picturesque suburbs with old churches, cottages and
houses of various sizes and ages. Villages within the
greater urban mass, one could say, and much sought
after for residence.

Altogether a very proud, historic place,
with something akin to Norwich about it in spite of
nearness to London.

CHELMSFORD

Chelmsford is towards the centre of the old
county of Essex and its is the county town despite
the obvious appeal and rivalry of Colchester.
Chelmsford in the last 30 years has grown enormously
as armies of commuters decide that here is a pleasant
country town with fast rail and road connections to
London and their workplaces, and so by the thousand
London families have moved out. Property was for
long a cheaper bet here in the country, though the
prices have risen inordinately in the last decade,
and the road traffic can be ferocious as people pile out
and into London daily. This was ever a travellers town
too on the route to the east coast ports and such major
towns as Ipswich.

The town is not only favoured residentially
with the influx of new commuters, but has its ancient
market functions including all manner of professional
services (such as legal and medical) for the county,
and a host of its own home grown industries. The
Marconi works come to mind, for here c1900 the pioneer
of wireless sent his first messages on the air waves,
and ever after substantial engineering factories have
been at work. The main roads, railway and rivers
contributed to economic life: the interesting
Chelmsford and Blackwater Navigation of the 1790s
linked the town to the open sea and led to a quay and

harbour quarter with wharves, warehouses and similar
premises.

The town has a number of distinguished
buildings but nowhere is there what one would call
a historic quarter thanks to the changes of the last
150 years destroying so much. The cathedral is
the old parish church raised not that long ago to
cathedral rank: it is still basically the church of
a prosperous regional centre, of flushwork, brick and
stone. The prominent feature is the late medieval
tower with its later needle spire and lantern.
The whole nave collapsed c1800 whilst alterations were
in hand, and had to be rebuilt totally - though the old
style was reproduced, and nicely. Lots of interesting
furnishings inside to be admired.

Chelmsford was, strangely enough, not a major
religious centre and only had the one house of friars
in the middle ages (Dominicans). It does have a good
run of Dissenting meeting houses and Dissent was ever
strong here and in the countryside from the 17th
century.

The shire hall of about 1790 is by local architect
John Johnson, who rebuilt the parish church, and this
time he used a noble classical facade in brick and
ashlar to produce a monumental piece.

PLenty of civic buildings have been provided
over the last 100 years including big new county hall,
town hall and so on. This is the centre for local history
of the county, and Essex record office was, when I was
an undergraduate, famous for its illustrious contributions
to research in the field.

Oaklands House is a 19th century villa in
lovely park which is a museum. Well worth a trip by
the visitor for its displays of local information on
history and traditional life.

Various once remote villages have been
swallowed up by Chelmsford as it expanded. Thus
Springfield, with the old county gaol, is one, and
Widford, with its Georgian buildings, is another.

Chelmsford was once notorious for the burning of
witches, mainly in the 17th century, I recall the
activities of the notorious Witchfinder General of
the 1640s being centred round here - Matthew Hopkins,
I think, was the man's name, who sent scores to their
death and was subject of a somewhat colourful and
lurid film 20 years ago ! he, of course, came to a bad
end !

BRAINTREE

        Braintree is astride the main roads
between Bishops Stortford and Colchester and Bury St
Edmunds to Chelmsford a junction of Roman
age and reason for the initial growth of this
country town. It is often listed with its small
neighbour Bocking as one town, formerly gaining wealth
from a market established in the 12th century and
from the income of mills including cloth works
throughout the middle ages and into the 17th century.
It was one of the eastern towns which benefited from
the arrival of the Huguenots of that century fleeing
persecution for their Protestant ways in France.
When cloth moved to Yorkshire and the north in the 18th
century, the local economy took a turn for the worst.

        The town was to some extent saved by the arrival
of the Courtauld family who set up a silk establishment
in Braintree in the 1800s, and expanded their concerns
over the course of that century. The railway
came in the 1840s and brought new economic developments
too.   Strangely enough it was also the Victorian
home to Crittall's windows, established by a man of that
name in Braintree and a considerable 20th century
employer.

        I first worked on the town's history thanks to
early contact with its most famous literary figure,
Nicholas Udall, vicar in the 1530s and 1540s and

author of RALPH ROISTER DOISTER, published in 1566
and a very early English masterpiece - Udall probably
wrote it 20 years later when head of Eton college,
when he was sacked for brutality !

Plenty of historic buildings as well as any
amount of Victorian and modern factory and housing
growth. Bradford Street took my eye with its medieval
properties and Georgian ones mixed in easy neighbourliness,
as should always be the case in a country town.
Several fine pubs and inns, many enjoyable houses and
cottages, with a parish church severely handled in
the 1860s but retaining an old chapel put up by
Udall in the 1540s.

MALDON

Maldon is sited where the Blackwater estuary
reaches right up to the river Chelmer and the land
not far out of Chelmsford. It is on rising land well
above the flat coastline and former marshland, and
was before Saxon times a place of consequence. King
Edward had a mint and fortress here to keep the Danes
in check in the 900s and it features in Domesday as
a borough or town. It was a constituency returning
2 MPs for 5 or 6 centuries, and curiously had its
franchise severely restricted   after the great reform
act of 1832 - a most unusual case of the opposite of
the desired effect occurring.

Maldon is something of a resort, sailing
centre and tourist town, with its own harbour, fishing and
pleasure craft, quay, various old inns and a network of
old alleys, paths and narrow roads which bear witness
to its ancient history. Just look at the quality of
the Moot Hall, the Blue Boar, the Swan and other larger
edifices ! PLenty of Georgian brick as well as more
homely timber and boarding from several centuries.

The various parish churches provide a great
deal of interest. St Peter's was made into a parish
library in the 1700s with just the tower remaining;
All Saints has a unique triangular tower to solve the

problem of a very awkward building. And it also has
a brilliantly decorated south aisle of particular
brilliance, and quite justly widely known. St Mary's
is a Norman structure much altered over the centuries,
and with interesting Tudor brickwork. It stands
near the Marine Parade and the great Marine Lake of
the 1900s, built for all manner of craft.

Beeleigh abbey is just out of town,
a house of Premonstratensian canons founded in
1180 and today represented by a fair amount of
masonry: the east claustral range with chapter
house, warming room, and reredorter for instance,
and mostly in a later house's fabric. A man on whom
I worked a deal often came here as head of the Order
in England - Bishop Redman in the late 15th and early
16th century, abbot of Shap not that far from where
I write these lines.

BRIGHTLINGSEA

Brightlingsea is on a virtual island site of
thousands of acres a few miles below Colchester and on
the way out to Clacton, but with just the one road
in and out of its remote area. It is another of those
Essex small ports which have had centuries of sailing
history but which today is reduced to the status of
pleasure boating centre. Then again it has its shell
fish and fishing businesses, for this coast is one of
the chief haunts of oysters. In the town near the
harbour and quay there used to be considerable boat
building activities of the traditional vehicles of these
coastal waters, the rigged barges or ketches of which
so few now remain.

The town made too the oyster smacks of 10 or
12 tons burden for the coastal work. Timber was in
constant use for building, and what you recall
about the town's architecture is its display of
carpentry in the boarded houses ranging from cottages
to substantial piles. The Beriffe family seem to have
been all-powerful for centuries, and the church is
full of their memorials. Their old home is the medieval
Jacobes Hall, all timber looking and ancient.
The parish church has a flint and flushwork tower of

quality, towards 100 feet high, and some curious items
inside the main building's walls: Roman bricks. This
was to some extent a heavily Romanised district thanks to
the influence of Colchester, and various Roman houses
and villas have been discovered in the district.
The church sits out of town on something of a hill;
you get a good viewpoint of the flat lands from it.
The town itself displays the sort of quaint old street
pattern that the tourists love, and alongside the
timbered properties are discreet Georgian houses and
businesses.

SOUTHEND

        Who would have guessed that such a remote,
unpromising, marshy, flat district in 1800 would have
grown by the 1980s into the main conurbation of
the county of Essex. From the villages of Leigh and
Prittlewell grew a town which, when we went, seemed
to attract most of London and the south east of England
to enjoy its holiday delights. Steamers used to ply up
and down the Thames which fronts the place, bringing
day trippers and longer stay folk in the early 19th
century, and using a small wooden jetty for the
purpose. I remember in EMMA, of the 1800s some
of the characters were placed by Jane Austen at South End
too.

        The pace of change quickened in the 1850s with
the first railway link, and the town rapidly developed
its facilities: things got going really fast in the
late Victorian years with a second, more direct rail route
from London which brought the trippers in by the thousands
each week in the season. This century the trippers have
continued to grow in numbers, but a vast burgeoning of
new residents has taken place as Londoners decided
either to retire here or to commute   to London
by rail or road. Thus this enormous settlement has
continued to expand.

Southend offers the total experience demanded
by holidaying families. It also offers things for the
student of historic towns. The cliff district has
a number of pre and early Victorian hotels and large
villas offering an object lesson in display with
lots of space inside; ironwork is plentifully on
view too. The pier is enormous, arguably one of the
longest at nearly 1½ miles right out to sea, and of
the 1890s and 1920s mostly, being extended and
refurbished each time. It is like a day out going on to
it alone !

In the north of the town is the airport and
Eastwood village with its fine   parish church that
appears to be a Norman fabric. Most interesting use of
medieval and later timber boarding in and on the church
adds character. The other older settlements also have
their places of interest amidst a vast ocean of
late Victorian and 20th century housing and industrial
estates.

Prittlewell has the remains of a Cluniac priory
of the middle ages, founded in the 1100s and colonised
by Lewes. It was a very rich body with 18 gifts of
presentation to parish churches (advowsons) and much land
and possessions. All that is left is a bit of the
cloisters and refectory, guest house and undercroft
mainly of the Norman and 15th century eras.
A few older cottages and houses are in the village
as it once was.

Leigh on Sea used to be a little fishing
place and it remains a historic focal point for
locals and visitors with old cottages and houses in
weatherboarding   ancient looking fishing boats and
their sheds, and a number of fine looking larger
houses from a more leisured era.

Of major buildings I suppose that one would
mention the mayor's residence, of Jacobean date called
Porters. Southchurch hall was a medieval moated manor
house now in other uses, and Thorpe Hall is a
Restoration property of suitably elegant size and
craftsmanship.

Shoebury and Shoeburyness are to the
eastern edge of the conurbation and looking out to
the distant continent with the enormous array of shipping
that comes by most days. Sheerness in Kent is due south
across the Thames estuary. These formerly old
settlements mainly have nice ancient Anglican parish
churches, occasional old cottages and houses, a very few
bigger domestic properties of age and consequence.

WITHAM

an old town. Since the 1940s the old centre has become
historic looking compared with the substantial new
housing and industrial estates of the place; not far
by fast main road or main railway to London of course, or
the Essex and Suffolk ports, and cheaper too for staff
and premises than the Great Wen.

        The traffic which used to flow through the
centre of Witham, running between Chelmsford and
Colchester, used to destroy any enjoyment of this old
town: it now has its bypass and things are much improved
as a result, and the tourists now flock in. It
was a Saxon settlement with defences against the
Danes provided by Alfred's son Edward, one of the kings
who stood up successfully to the new invaders in the
10th century. Chipping (that is market in Saxon)
Hill was the old centre by the great earthworks of the
Saxons but the town moved to its present axis of the
old A12 or Newland Street.

        This is a street packed full of old properties:
the predominant feel is of the Georgian red brick
era of the 18th century, and there are scores of
these attractive old properties here and off in the
side streets as well as a few older fabrics to be
admired. Timber framed places suggest late medieval
and 16th century dates here, and there are several old
inns which served the ceaseless flow of travellers
over the centuries before and after the coaching age.

        The parish church is medieval and of several
styles of architecture, all of them blending in fairly
well to create the sort of structure one would want in

BURNHAM ON CROUCH

GREAT DUNMOW

Burnham is on the river Crouch where it
emerges from the land into the sea and forms vast expanses
of marsh and mud flat near Foulness Island: there is
still a feeling of utter remoteness in parts of the
district though the Southend conurbation is not far distant.

The town was centre for the remote communities of
the coastline which covers thousands of acres, and
at the old quayside there used to be considerable local
and coastal traffic from the middle ages right into last
century when good roads and above all railways killed it
all off. Today, and for a century, it is mostly
yachting and pleasure craft but occasionally an old
sailing barge complete with rigging and sail comes in and
ties up.

It is an attractive small town centre with a
mixture of modern and Victorian properties including
clock tower but which never manage to spoil the older
properties - Georgian brick houses and shops, weather
boarded cottages and larger structures, often of
indeterminate dates . The parish church is well out of
the centre and not that distinguished really: its
vicar was chaplain in attendance to Admiral Nelson when
he died at Trafalgar - a funny thing to remember I
suppose for the tourists !

Great Dunmow is about halfway along the main route
between Bishops Stortford and Braintree, but is now
bypassed and gains accordingly. It sits by the little
river Chelmer with slightly rising hilly land on either
side working down to Chelmsford, and has the distinction
of being just down the road from the rapidly burgeoning
airport of Stanstead. Little Dunmow, a far smaller
settlement, is the other way out of town.

Great Dunmow was a 13th century market town serving
the wide rural district especially to the north, and
grew up along the old Roman roads. Nearby was the
Augustinian priory founded in 1106 by Geoffrey Baynard,
which though small has left amongst the best documentary
records for any house of the Order. What remains of it
is very interesting: a long narrow chancel which serves as
parish church to Little Dunmow.

Great Dunmow has many good buildings of both brick
and timber framing: rows of cottages most picturesque and
Georgian, vaguely classical, houses and businesses which
show a modest provincial wealth for centuries. The parish
church has a noble 15th century tower, a rare medieval
gallery in the south aisle, and late medieval timbered
vicarage.

Clock House has a 1651 clock turret and bell
housing with a house of the previous century , and home to
Sir George Beaumont, the first patron of the illustrious
John Constable. You can easily follow the road along
little byways up to Saffron Walden to enjoy the sort of
countryside well known to these men in the late 18th and
early 19th century: quite a few of the properties in the
villages along it were there in that era too.

HARWICH

Harwich is a door to Europe for the entire
county, and sits facing across to its rival port of
Felixstowe in the next county. It grew up in the middle
ages on a narrow peninsula of land where the rivers
Stour and Orwell run into the North Sea, and some of
the quaint and picturesque streets of the old quarter
remain today to be enjoyed. You actually depart from
Parkstone usually so the old town is often missed,
which is a pity.

Harwich always suffered drastically from the
cycles of depression and boom. The coast needed lots
of protection from erosion too and these were only made
final and permanent last century. It was fortified
with a substantial wall and gates in the middleages
and had a Tudor fort   : its naval dockyards were
prosperous then, but rivalry with Sheerness led to
decline and a general low ebb of trade in the 18th
century despite its fine c1660 expansion as harbour and
docks.

The town retains many interesting and old
buildings though these usually mix in with less
satisfactory Victorian and modern ones. Thus you can
enjoy old pubs and inns which are quite atmospheric
of the old sailing days of the seadogs et al ! Old
warehouses, shops and houses mingle various materials

and dates and styles of architecture: thus Georgian
and classical brick sits by timber framed late
medieval jettied, plaster and stucco with weather
boarding and gables. The town of course has a true
seafaring pedigree and much is made of such connections
as the MAYFLOWER .

Dovercourt was a resort creation of the 1850s
when John Bagshaw encouraged others to invest with
him in creating a town which was to rival other
creations of the railway age in providing holidays.
Not that much is old of course, and late Victorian and
modern development has taken over and swallowed early
developments. A great deal to see in the way of
lighthouses and their history hereabouts too.

HALSTEAD

About 12 miles to the west of Colchester is
Halstead, market town set on important cross roads
and with a long steeply sloping High Street. It was
well known for its crepe and silk manufacturies over the
centuries, and there is a famous weather boarded mill
on the riverside which was was opened in the 1820s
by Courtaulds. This factory complex presents a
most appealing sight complete with buildings for other
purposes and workers ' cottages too.

The town provides plenty of interest to the
tourist: bargeboarded houses, weather boarded cottages,
red brick town houses, classical Georgian and Victorian
 variety making the townscape a nice walk. The church
is associated with the Bourchier family, one of those
great noble dynasties of such note in the middle ages
but whose names are now best known through streets
named after them ! This church of St Andrew's is
a flint structure which is mainly a Victorian rebuild
job, but with old bits worked into it. Amongst a
wealth of monuments and furnishings are the rather
grand Bourchier memorials: plans to make the parish
church into a collegiate ones foundered due to the Black
Death which so devastated these rich districts in 1349.

BRENTWOOD

WOODFORD AND WOODFORD GREEN

Just on the far, east side, of the M25 is
Brentwood, and therefore just inside the present
Essex boundary. It was an old settlement which expanded
as coaching and travelling trade grew   and today it
is a substantial industrial and housing place: not only
does it have its quota of commuters, but many homegrown
industries for local workers. The population pressure
indeed has been growing ever more urgent as this
century has progressed.

The town has, besides its vast new
building complexes, some of its old timbered structures
remaining and especially its old inns and hostelries.
The new parish church is far larger than the old
(now ruined but most picturesque in its gardens)
church - especially with its lofty spire and tower in
nicest Victorian style. The local grammar school was
an unusual, Marian, foundation of 1557, when the nation
had supposedly lapsed back into Roman ways briefly,
and the founder Sir Anthony Browne, wanted an RC
establishment for teaching local boys. Ingatestone
hall, in best red brick which suggests the late 16th
century, is the best period property, and now used
for exhibitions and displays - it comes complete with
priest and hiding holes too !

Woodford used to have a pleasant and quite
distinguished parish church but I remember it being burned
down some years ago and replaced by a modern structure.
It is anyway not so much the buildings as the people that
one recalls about this district of the new London borough
of Redbridge, set in north London with Waltham Forest to
its west, Havering on the east, and Newham and Barking to
the south. The district does have a number of fine,
detached, classical villas of the 18th and early
19th centuries: Highams, of the 1760s, Hurst House of
50 years earlier (and arguably the finest property of
the borough), and the old parsonage, being just examples
of the best properties. Today there has been enormous
growth in the town of Waltham, with most open spaces
filled in for houses that have burgeoned forth over
the last 30 years.

People of prominence include John Barnardo,
famous founder of the eponymous organisation that cares
for homeless and orphaned children- and his life is
one of especial interest, for his father was Jewish and
his mother Irish and he himself was born in Dublin in
the Hungry 1840s (as they were called). After deciding to
become a missionary, Barnardo trained as a physician too
to help his work, and in London of the 1860s found his
role in life helping the homeless children. Here in
Woodford were set up early homes for the children thanks

to the wealth of his wife and father in law who bought
the land and paid for the properties: the name and
places live on.

Interestingly William Morris, founder of the
famous Pre-Raphaelite Brethren of the 1850s, was raised
here after his family came to Woodford when he was 6
about 1840. It is strange to think that this semi-rural
place in those days should cast such influence over its
residents like Morris. Robert Raikes, of an earlier
generation, is (like the Morris seniors) buried here:
he was a Gloucester man and his early work in that
city was amongst the rabble of children of the
Georgian period who made Sundays misery for the rest
of society. Popular schooling and Sunday schooling
were his forte, and his great energy and skills were
in the field of promoting and organising these.

Coventry Patmore, who was an Anglican
clergyman and respected poet of the Victorian years
was born and raised in Woodford of the 1820s and 1830s.
His was a circle which embraced Tennyson and John
Ruskin, but he left the Establishment in the 1860s
and became RC - all this after his THE ANGEL IN THE
HOUSE, a series of poems about married love and life,
a sort of praise of it all, and for which he researched
for years in the British Library and Museum. He was
formerly a canon of St Paul's and inherited wealth too.
I had to read his work when working on the history of
women (!) in Britain - he did not impress me !

I suspect Woodford and Woodford Green are more for
living in than for tourists, but very interesting places
they have proved to be for the literary set.

ILFORD

Ilford, according to maps of 150 years ago,
was a rural community well away from London, and
populated by gentlemen, their families, servants,
tenant farmers and nurserymen (for this was fertile
land). The settlement burgeoned forth with the
effects of the railways after the 1830s, and gradually it
became a substantial Victorian settlement - but according
to maps between the world wars, one with more than
its share of open green spaces, and not linked with its
neighbours. It now forms the southern, very built up,
district of Redbridge, against Barking and Newham,
and it is mostly a late Victorian and 20th century
centre of industries, enormous housing and business
estates, main roads and shopping districts.

Its chief claims to fame in historic circles
are a diverse lot. First there is the famous
library, a product of the 1960s when those ghastly
mistakes were made by so many town councils. In this
case instead the new library was a brilliant essay
in design success by Frederick Gibberd, a circular
building topped by cupola - a delight to see it.
Then there is the old Roman site, now with next to
nothing on show, but at one time important.
Valentines Park retains a c1700 mansion, home to the
council today and with lovely gardens.

And the Norman almshouses, at one time called
St Mary's Hospital, and now mainly 17th and 19th
century architecture, are as good an example of
the type as is to be found in the region. I suppose that
its chapel is the gem complete with early medieval
masonry and in daily use.

BARKING AND DAGENHAM

Dagenham of course is best known for its
For motor car factory, but there is rather more to it
than this, admittedly substantial, employer.
The district, much of its fields and open land,
was something of a model for new housing after the
Great War when there was a shortage of homes for the
rapidly expanding city of London: so in the 1920s the
London County Council bought 3,000 acres spread about
the place, and up went 27,000 properties to form one
of the world's largest council estates ! One cannot say
now that it looks that good to a visitor, but for the
between the wars era it was a star set against the
city centre alternatives. And of course there
are enormous areas of industrial development too.
However, historically speaking, this is all new, and
Dagenham has a long past.

Dagenham was all estates and manors into the
19th century. The parish church of St Peter and
St Paul suggests this with its show of monuments
and tablets on the old parish, a notable array and
quite a surprise to thsoe who only know of Fords.
The church is of the 1800s mainly, with some medieval
fabric. Sadly many of the old big houses were
demolished between the wars, though their parks were
occasionally made into free parks for the public -
all to the good. Valence manor house I suppose is
the star left out of all the mansions, and well worth
keeping.

Dagenham had, into last century, extensive marshaland, now given over to industry, docks and similar, and Hainault forest, also largely gone thanks to intensive clearance of the timber and land improvement.

Barking used to have a famous abbey, a house of Benedictine nuns founded in the 970s by King Edgar and St Dunstan, leaders of the religious revival of the time. It had actually been a 7th century house but destroyed by the Danes in the 9th century; the house flourished in the middle ages, and the abbess was a peer of the realm in her own right. The abbey church was larger than Rochester cathedral and bearing in mind that 3 queens and 2 princesses were buried here, it had influential friends and great income. Barking had the distinction of being the 3rd wealthiest nunnery in the entire nation; the parish church was built in the middle ages inside the abbey precincts, which was most rare.

Not much exists of the once great house: just the curfew gate house and odd bits, but the parish church remains, and a splendid one it is too: 13th century and later, packed with monuments and interesting furnishings, and by the river Roding. This river went into Barking CReek and the Thames, and for generations local folk were mainly engaged either in fishing or in both fishing and farming.   It is hard to imagine a fishing fleet putting out each week, but that is exactly   what happened !

Modern Barking of course is representative of all London: packed with people, roads, railway, shopping districts and centres, housing and industrial estates by the score, and seemingly endless urban growth to fill nearly every free inch.

BASILDON AND BILLERICAY

You have to look hard to find historic parts to these two towns so close to each other today, but they do have old and interesting buildings within their daily expanding cores.   Billericay was a part of the medieval parish of Great Burstead (which ironically sits between the two towns now) and has its own church of the 18th century with a c1500 brick tower and a number of old cottages and houses of about that date round the vicinity of the church and down the High Street. To walk round them today is instructive as it is sad, for here are some fine examples of late medieval townscape yet far more were knocked down this century.

The granting of market status to Billericay brought growth and income. The town has Mayflower history too since a number of the locals went on that seminal American journey c1619. The actual site of the town is good, higher land surrounded by lowland - hence a desire to get away from marsh and flooding. Billericay has its Georgian buildings too, again in brick and with true provincial restraint and dignity.

Basildon was conceived as a new town after the last world war, covering 7 existing parishes with a scattered population of 25,000 but having a final size of 140,000 after 30 years. Of the historic bits and pieces left in the new ocean of modernity are the churches at Vange, Pitsea and Basildon - the last named the most interesting.

CLACTON

COGGESHALL

Clacton on Sea is a solid Victorian creation of
the days when the railway arrived and people had both
the time and money (and inclination !) to descend on
what was then a remote district.   The villages of
Great and Little Clacton were medieval villages with old
churches, something of a market function, and have
a number of older properties remaining despite the
vast amount of building in the last century.

With a particularly nice stretch of beach
the coastal growth of a new Clacton began c1870, and
with this century rocketted: from humble beginnings of
odd hotels, guest houses, pier and a few shops of the
late Victorian era, Clacton grew to become a large and
prosperous resort and retirement centre for Londoners.
This is what it has remained.

The amount of sheer entertainment that goes on is
quite astonishing: and all to attract and to keep the
tourists !

Coggeshall is a small country town now bypassed
by the old Roman road from Braintree to Colchester.
It is a historic centre packed with old buildings that
attract tourists by the thousand. It was a centre of
medieval wealth from cloth and wool which shows in
the astounding Paycocke's House, now a National
Trust property and a brilliant exposition of Essex
Tudor timber houses. The decoration is especially
rich, showing a frieze of foliage, intricate carved
heads, jettied upper storey, linenfold panelling,
lovely fireplaces - in fact the lot !

It is not alone in its beauty and there are
as many historic houses and properties for a town of
this size as anywhere that I know. These include the
Woolpack inn of the later medieval centuries, a 15th
century parish church restored to its former elegance after
war damage in 1940, and weather boarded clock tower
and watch bell of hexagonal shape. Market Hill, East
Street, Stoneham Street, and Bridge and Church Streets
display the wealth of the town in the late middle ages
and 16th century: quite remarkable to see so many
lovingly cared for survivors !

GRAYS

WALTON ON THE NAZE

        Grays of course is the name given to a
considerable conurbation on the south Essex coast
not far out of London - or at least it is in maps !
In fact it embraces West Thurrock, Little Thurrock, and
East Thurrock or Grays. Riverside, Thames,
development rules, with any amount of dockland and
harbourside buildings as has been the case in this
flat, marshy, tedious landscape for centuries.
The name Thurrock actually comes from an ancient
Saxon word for the bottom of a ship or boat where the
dirt collects ! Even today this remains Essex though
the London boundary creeps very near.

        Grays has a medieval church including
Norman work but drastically altered last century
(as usual !). The town keeps a few older houses, inns
and business premises, but not that many. Little
Thurrock has those peculiar, and locally famous,
Dane or Dene Holes which are deep shafts apparently
for prehistoric man and offering interest and
danger to all !

        West Thurrock keeps a few old premises too,
including a medieval parish church, but the scale of
office and industrial buildings is vast and they dwarf
everything. Purfleet is in this quarter, right against
both Thames and London boundary. Local chalk deposits
were much quarried for industries over the centuries.

        The settlement on the nose, naze or ness
is one of the county's resorts facing over to Europe
and frequently subjected to inundations by the
sea. It has a formidably long 800 foot pier to allow
boats in to a few feet of water, dangerous rocks and
approaches , and a lighthouse of the 1700s. The pier
was of c1830 and used by visiting steam pacquets
as they were then called, but the little resort never
quite took off in the manner of some rather more
successful ones.

        Fine beaches, sheltered sunbathing, cliffs,
all the amusements you could want for a day out,
characterise Walton: it bears little relationship with
the Domesday settlement however, and as it developed
piecemeal in the 19th century, not much in the way of
good architecture came into being. Plenty of modern
housing too. The old settlement of course was finally
engulfed by the sea in 1798: the only compensation I
suppose concerns the fossils around here.

ILLUSTRATIONS

No. 32.—Vol. I.

CHURCH BELLS

EDITED BY J. ERSKINE CLARKE, M.A.

SATURDAY, August 5, 1871.

One Penny.

'Ring out the False : Ring in the True.'

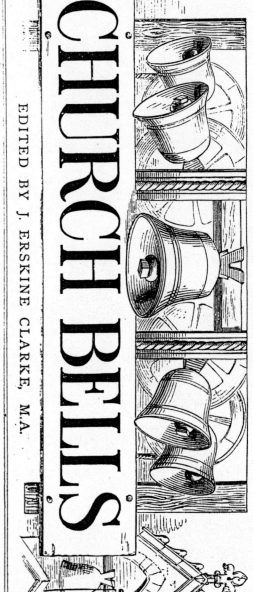

NORWICH CATHEDRAL.

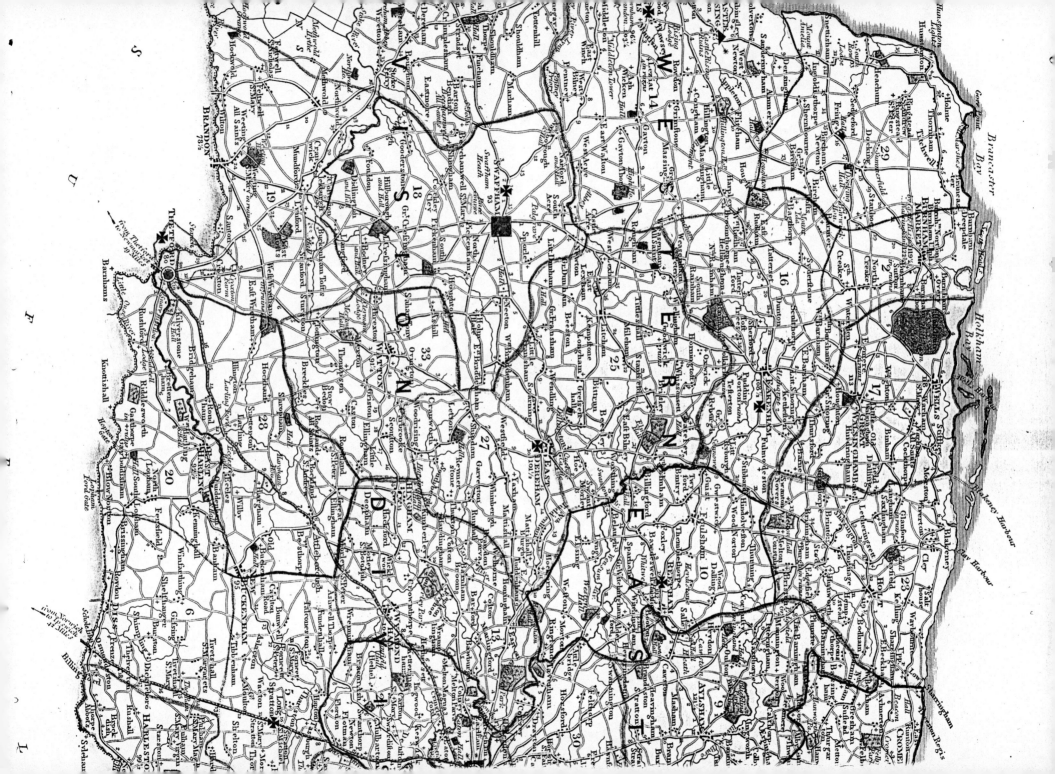

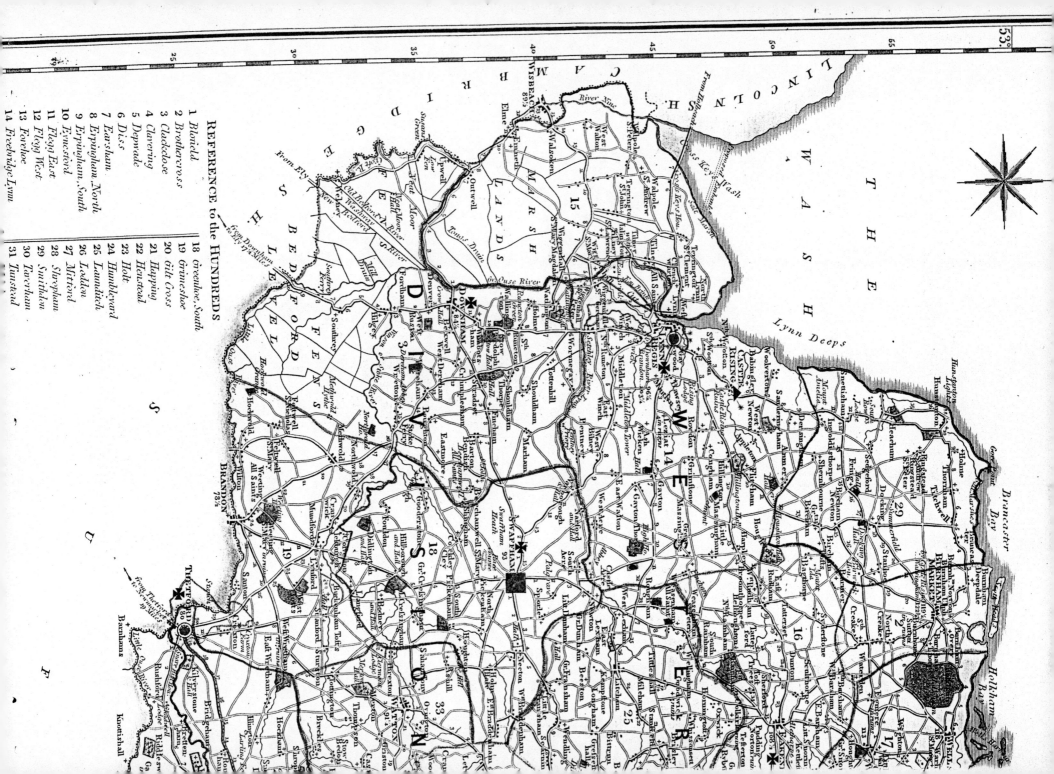

REFERENCE to the HUNDREDS

1 Blofield	18 Greenhoe, South
2 Brothercross	19 Grimeshoe
3 Clackclose	20 Gilt Cross
4 Clavering	21 Happing
5 Depwade	22 Henstead
6 Diss	23 Holt
7 Earsham	24 Humbleyard
8 Erpingham North	25 Launditch
9 Erpingham, South	26 Loddon
10 Eynesford	27 Mitford
11 Flegg East	28 Shropham
12 Flegg West	29 Smithdon
13 Forehoe	30 Taverham
14 Freebridge-Lynn	31 Tunstead

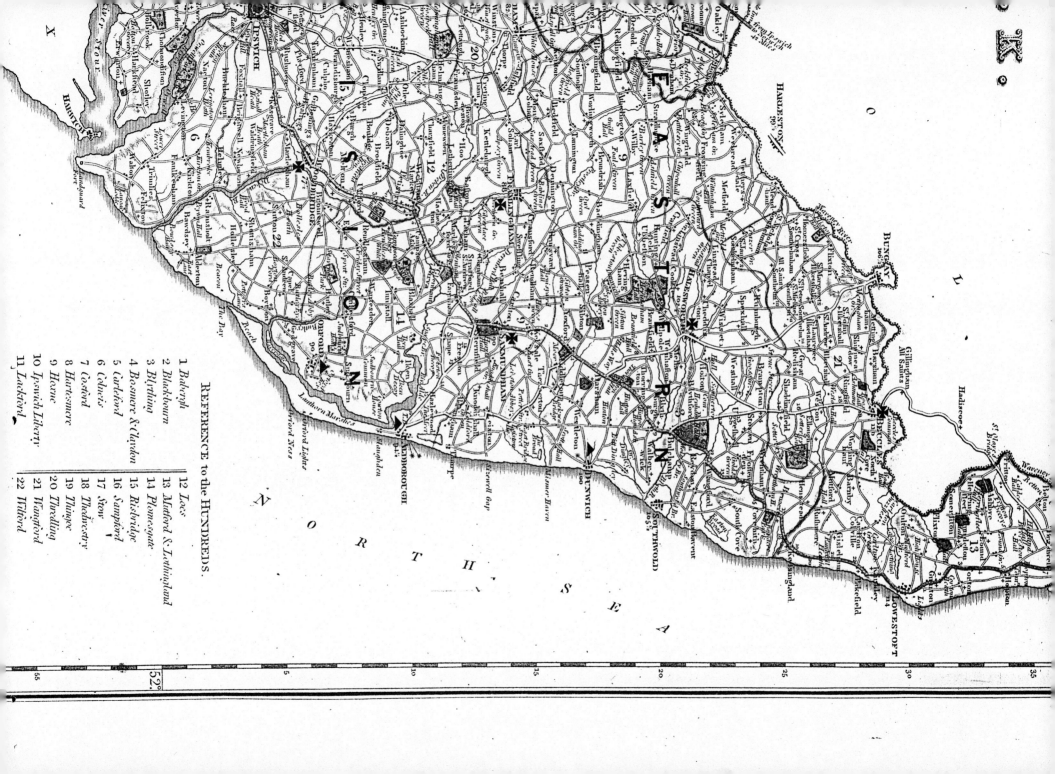

REFERENCE to the HUNDREDS.

1 Babergh
2 Blackbourn
3 Blything
4 Bosmere & Claydon
5 Carleford
6 Colneis
7 Cosford
8 Hartesmere
9 Hoxne
10 Ipswich Liberty
11 Lackford
12 Loes
13 Mitford & Lothingland
14 Plomesgate
15 Risbridge
16 Sampford
17 Stow
18 Thedwestry
19 Thingoe
20 Thredling
21 Wangford
22 Wilford

HARLESTON

BUNGAY

SOUTHWOLD

BECCLES

LOWESTOFT

IPSWICH

HARWICH

WOODBRIDGE

ALDBOROUGH

DUNWICH

EAST SUFFOLK

NORTH SEA

52°